WORLD EDUCATION SERIES

Reforms and Restraints in Modern French Education

World education series

GENERAL EDITOR: DR BRIAN HOLMES
Reader in Comparative Education
Institute of Education
University of London

Education and Development
in Latin America
Laurence Gale

Education in Communist China
R. F. Price

Reforms and Restraints in Modern French Education

W. R. FRASER
Woodbrooke College, Birmingham

London
ROUTLEDGE & KEGAN PAUL

First published 1971
by Routledge & Kegan Paul Ltd
Broadway House, 68–74 Carter Lane,
London EC4V 5EL

Printed in Great Britain by
Richard Clay (The Chaucer Press) Ltd,
Bungay, Suffolk
and set in Ehrhardt 11 pt

ISBN 0 7100 7174 4

Contents

Part One: The School System

Part Two: The Politics of Education

Contents

Part Three: Educational Problems

Tables & Diagrams

Diagrams

World education series

The volumes in the *World Education Series* will treat national systems of education and, where appropriate, features of different systems within a particular region. These studies are intended to meet the needs of students of comparative education in university departments and schools of education and colleges of education and will supplement the growing volume of literature in the field. They may also appeal to a wider lay audience interested in education abroad.

As an area study of a national system each volume presents an accurate, reasonably up-to-date account of the most important features of the educational system described. Among these are the ways in which the school system is controlled, financed and administered. Some account is given of the various kinds of school within the system and the characteristics of each of them. The principles of curriculum organization and some aspects of teacher education are outlined. Of more interest, however, is the analysis which is made in each volume of the unique national characteristics of an educational system, seen in the context of its history and the sociological, economic and political factors which have influenced in the past and continue now to influence educational policy.

The assumption behind the series is, however, that common socio-economic and educational problems find unique expression in a particular country of region, and that a brief analysis of some major national issues will reveal similarities and differences. Thus, while in each case the interpretation of policies and practices is based on the politics of education, the interpretative emphasis will vary from one country to another.

The framework of analysis for each volume is consequently the same, attention being drawn in the first section to the legal basis of educational provision, followed in the second section by an analysis of the political considerations which have and do influence the formulation, adoption and implementation of policy. The role of political parties is described where appropriate and the influence of the church or churches on policy examined. Attention too is given to the activities of pressure groups at national, regional and local levels. Changing industrial, urban and familial patterns are used to show how educational needs are in process of change and what difficulties arise when innovations are attempted. Again, each author touches on the extent to which economic resources affect the implementation of policy. The analysis relates principally to the twenty-year period between 1945 and 1965 but relevant aspects of the pre-Second World War period are described and the chains of events are seen in historical perspective.

Finally, in the third section some account is given of problems which arise within the educational system itself. Those which appear to the author of particular interest and importance have been treated in some depth. Others have been referred to so that readers may consult other sources of information if they wish. Broad problem areas in education have, however, been identified. The points of transition within a system between the first and second and between the second and third stages of education give rise to problems of selection and allocation. Under conditions of expansion, created by explosions of population and aspirations, traditional solutions are often thought to be no longer adequate. The attempts made to meet these new situations are described. So too are the relationships and debates about them, between the various types of school at different levels of education. For example what are the possibilities of transfer between academic, general and technical/vocation schools at the second stage of education? And where these different types have been replaced by some form of common or comprehensive school what kinds of differentiation exist within the single school? At the third level of higher education what relationships exist between institutions providing general education, professional training and research opportunities? In some systems a form of dual control is growing up with the universities retaining much of their traditional autonomy and the technological institutes and teacher education institutions increasingly feeling the influence of government agencies. Again, after a process of differentiation in course content in the first stage of higher education there is now a tendency for the first year (or two) of college or university work to be regarded as a preparatory year (or years) with common or somewhat similar courses of studies for all students.

Particular attention has been paid to the problems which arise in the area of teacher education. Movements in most countries are in the direction of bringing together the previously separate systems of training for elementary and secondary school teachers. Common entrance prerequisites to different training institutions may now be required. Where this is not yet the case training colleges usually make it possible for students to obtain, during the course of their studies, a certificate which grants entry to the university and highest (in prestige and status) forms of teacher education. The place of teacher education in the structure of higher education is, in short, discussed in each of the volumes. So are debates about curricular content and methods of certification.

Finally, some attention is given to the interaction of the schools and other social agencies. Among these the health services, youth organizations, the family, the Church, industry and commerce have been regarded as important. Where special note is not taken of such institutions the impact they have in the schools is dealt with throughout the volume as a whole.

The framework in short is intended to facilitate cross-cultural studies through the series as a whole. Basic educational legislation is referred to in the belief that it gives the most reliable and valid source of national goals or aims in education. The problems of putting these into effective action are socio-economic-political and educational. Comparisons can be made, therefore, between the aims of education as expressed in national legislation and between the main factors which inhibit or facilitate practical provisions in accordance with these aims.

BRIAN HOLMES
General Editor

General editor's introduction

The quality of French education is world renowned. The apparent orderliness of its system of centralized administration has attracted much attention. The principles on which it is based are clear and logical. These features tend to disguise the complexities of an educational system which, like most others in Europe, has been the subject of much controversy since the end of the Second World War. French reformers have been dissatisfied more with the practice than with the theories on which it has been traditionally based.

It is useful in an attempt to understand the politics of reform to view present debates against some of the principles enunciated prior to, during and shortly after the Revolution. In 1763 La Chalotais published his *Essai d'Education Nationale ou Plan d'Études pour la Jeunesse* in which he urged the establishment of a national system of education free from clerical interference. Throughout the nineteenth century the State–Church struggle for control raged. It was not until the 1880s that legislation introduced by Jules Ferry laicized elementary education and, incidentally, made it free and compulsory. Even today, although much of the heat was taken out of the debate by the Debré reforms of 1959, the provision of public funds to church schools may still arouse the suspicion and hostility of anti-clerics in France.

Several detailed plans for a comprehensive system of education were formulated during the revolutionary period. Of these it is against the one presented to the Constituent Assembly by Condorcet in 1792 that present-day debates regarding the structure of the French school system can be understood. Condorcet proposed to create a system of universal primary schools in which all pupils would become acquainted with their civic rights and learn to discharge their civic duties responsibly. Primary schools for all were to be followed by a succession of institutions, admission to which was to be on the basis of merit. Thus an aristocracy of talent was to be selected and educated for national leadership. The *grandes écoles* epitomize the care taken by the founders of the French republican system of education to ensure that the nation had trained cadres of professional workers at the highest levels.

Today, the élitist character of French education is being questioned. The Algiers Commission which met before the end of the Second World War and the Langevin–Wallon plan published shortly after created a new interest in reform proposals which had been debated in the twenties and thirties to democratize education and enable it to meet modern economic needs by replacing selection for secondary education at eleven by a process of guidance and orientation over the first period of the second stage of education. Between 1945 and 1959 several attempts were made to introduce legislation designed to increase the flexibility of the traditional structure. Mr Fraser has admirably analysed in a previous book— *Education and Society in Modern France*—the obstacles which were placed in the way of reform. In this volume he summarizes the changes which occurred in the earlier period and pays special attention to problems of reform in the sixties.

The writings of the eighteenth-century encyclopedists established principles of curriculum development which are still debated. They stressed the importance of scientific knowledge and the value of modern languages in face of the traditional prestige of Greek and Latin. The relative merits of the various school subjects were debated throughout the nineteenth and into the twentieth centuries. Recent attempts to upgrade technical studies at the second and third levels of education are symptomatic of the high status still enjoyed by the classical languages and, in a somewhat lower position, the pure sciences. Nevertheless, the question is of 'relative merit' for the broad curriculum in the academic schools of France reflects encyclopedists' views of knowledge.

This academic tradition is perhaps best exemplified in the *lycées*. Thirty of these were provided for in the Fourcroy law of 1802. They were to be maintained at State expense and their curriculum was to include everything which pertained to a liberal education. The quality of the *lycées*, the power of those who teach in them and justifiable pride in their achievements make it difficult to introduce in France educational reforms which may impair the reputation of these famous schools.

Similar considerations stand in the path of administrative reform.

Napoleon's Imperial University was founded by the laws of 1806 and 1808, and included teachers at all levels of education and in all kinds of institutions. This corporation was dependent on the State and had the monopoly of education. Napoleon's hope was that there should be a teaching body with definitely recognized principles, one of which should be that members of the corporation should not be subjected to political interference. Much of the stability in French education, in spite of political upheavals, can be ascribed to the effective realization of this important concept. The power of the educationists and their independence has, however, made administrative reform difficult. Within the bureaucracy power is not as concentrated as is sometimes imagined. From its inception the power of the central ministry was balanced by the authority of rectors as heads of the Academies throughout the country. Each rector is administrative head, not only of the university in his region but of the school system as a whole. Again local control over primary and elementary schools contrasts with the ability of Ministry of Education officials to influence secondary school policies. There have also developed sharp differences of effective control at all levels between higher, secondary, elementary and technical education. Vested interests within this complex system of administrative control have made its reform difficult.

Mr Fraser deals with these issues in a case study which will be of interest to readers who wish to study French education, but should also appeal to a wider public who want to know more about the politics of educational reform. Four issues emerge very clearly—the position of Catholic schools, the reorganization of the selective structure of the school system, the reform of the curriculum and the realignment of central and regional agencies of administration. These are problems of educational reform debated everywhere. How the French have attempted to solve them makes fascinating reading. In France the Langevin–Wallon proposals provided as important a basis of reform as did the 1944 Education Act in England and Wales. Politics, economic conditions and the power of educationists delayed the passing of major legislation in France, yet the processes of change are instructive.

Mr Fraser surveys them in a lucid manner. He is well qualified to do so and to interpret the trends and future possibilities of development by virtue of his close acquaintance with France, his intimate knowledge of the language and the scholarly study he has made of French education over a long period of years.

The French experience, which Mr Fraser analyses, has been widely debated. Many countries, in attempting to meet their own problems, have looked to France for inspiration. Of particular interest are the attempts made to introduce a period of orientation and guidance at the second stage of education designed to postpone selection and vocational choice. The systematic collection of the data of planning, and the plans themselves, have attracted attention. The efforts made by the French authorities to raise the status of technical education, prolong compulsory education and reform the examination system have lessons for reformers everywhere. Not least the impact of student opinion on reform, admirably discussed by Mr Fraser, illustrates aspects of French life which owes much, paradoxically it may seem, to an educational system which has promoted intellectual excellence, allowed individualism to flourish, and yet has played a significant part in unifying France and making French men and women uniquely French.

BRIAN HOLMES

Preface

This study is in a sense a successor to my earlier book, *Education and Society in Modern France*, and deals chiefly with events that have taken place and currents that have run more strongly in the decade 1961–71.

But while this book is chronologically up to date, its main purpose is not so much to be recent as to invite an interpretation of what has happened and of what is still developing.

As such, it takes its place in the World Education Series under the general editorship of Dr Brian Holmes—to whom I am indebted for encouragement through a longer period of gestation than we foresaw —and its plan owes much to the editor's expertise in the methodology of comparative education.

I am especially grateful for the assistance given by M. Marcel Leherpeux and his colleagues in the Institut Pédagogique National where I have always found knowledgeable educationists willing to talk with me and to correspond afterwards. And I should like to express my warm thanks to my family for support during the vicissitudes of authorship and to Mrs Joan Tyers for sympathetically retyping many not too legible drafts.

W.R.F.

Glossary

académie   one of twenty-three regional divisions of France, each being the seat of a university or group of universities and being administered by a *recteur*.

agrégé   the holder of a title of distinction called *agrégation* which is granted in some academic fields of study (law, pharmacy, medicine) and to those graduate teachers who have succeeded in a severely competitive examination in their specialist subject.

baccalauréat   final secondary school examination; and the certificate awarded for success in that examination, giving access to a university; officially it is a bachelor's degree granted by the Minister of National Education.

brevet d'études professionnelles   a certificate granted to pupils passing an examination after two years of vocational studies beyond the first cycle of general education (four years) in a secondary school.

certificat d'aptitude pédagogique   the certificate awarded to primary school teachers on completion of their course in an *école normale*.

certificat d'aptitude professionnelle   generic term referring to any one of a large number of kinds of certificate similarly granted to those who have pursued studies in a technical college preparatory to taking up a trade or craft.

classe de sixième   the first class of the secondary school, classes being numbered thereafter in descending order; this class has three sections corresponding to the presumed ability of the pupils.

classe de transition   the third (slowest) stream of the *classe de sixième*.

collège d'enseignement général (*CEG*)   secondary school offering general studies, one foreign language and practical classes for four years.

collège d'enseignement secondaire (*CES*) secondary school offering all the options made available in the first cycle (four years) of secondary studies, viz. a classical section, two modern sections and a practical section.

concours competitive examination for admission to an institution, or for a qualification, or for appointment to a post.

cours complémentaire the name given before 1959 to the courses now offered by a *collège d'enseignement général*; they were taught to pupils who had not been selected for academic secondary education.

culture générale a frequently proclaimed goal in French education: that degree of understanding and of skill in manipulating symbols and concepts which enables the well-educated person to converse intelligently on a wide range of topics, to approach new problems flexibly and to acquire new skills on a sound basis of general education.

cycle d'observation et d'orientation the first four years of the secondary school leading to guidance offered by teachers and representatives of the school medical and social services to parents on the basis of the pupils' record and observed performance.

école maternelle nursery school for children from two to six years of age; not part of their obligatory schooling.

école normale training school for primary school teachers; there is one for men and one for women in each of the ninety administrative *départements* of France; they are boarding establishments, admitting pupils by competitive examination for four years from the age of fifteen or at the post-*baccalauréat* level for two years of professional training.

enseignement élémentaire primary schooling for pupils from six to eleven years of age.

faculté department of a university concerned with one main field of studies, e.g. Arts, or Medicine, or Science.

grandes écoles establishments of higher education to which admission is gained by competitive examination after two or three years of study beyond the *baccalauréat* level, e.g. Ecole Normale Supérieure (for secondary school teachers), Ecole

Polytechnique (for army officers and engineers), Ecole Nationale Supérieure des Mines (for mining engineers), Ecole Nationale Supérieure des Ponts et Chaussées (for civil engineers), Ecole Nationale d'Administration.

instituteur/institutrice primary school teacher who, after passing the *baccalauréat* examination, undergoes two years of training in an *école normale*.

licence the first post-school degree awarded in a university, usually after three or four years of study.

lycée a secondary school offering a full complement of courses up to the *baccalauréat*; some *lycées* also offer advanced courses to prepare pupils for entry to the *Grandes Ecoles*; the first cycle of studies in a *lycée* may gradually be transferred to a college of secondary education in the nineteen-seventies, leaving the *lycée* proper consisting only of the upper classes.

maîtrise the next academic degree awarded to those who have pursued studies beyond the level of the *licence*.

professeur (*a*) the occupant of a university chair, already possessing a doctorate degree; (*b*) a graduate holding also the certificate of aptitude for teaching in secondary schools (*capès*), or for teaching in technical schools (*capet*); (*c*) the holder of a university diploma who has also gained the certificate of aptitude for teaching in colleges of general education (*CAPCEG*).

recteur the Minister's representative in the *académie*, chancellor of the universities in that region.

tiers temps pédagogique a division of the primary school timetable, introduced in 1969, into three main parts; fifteen hours a week for basic subjects such as French and mathematics; six hours for history, geography, nature studies and singing; and six hours for physical activity and outdoor sports.

Université (*a*) the whole system of education envisaged as a coherent entity; (*b*) a combination of higher education units for teaching and research representing various disciplines of study and recognized by the Minister as a university under the terms of the Higher Education Orientation Law of November 1968.

PART ONE

The school system

I

Evolution and mission

Legislation for reform

Examining the succession of laws, decrees and ordinances that reformers have written in an attempt to encourage mutation in the French Education System is sometimes a confusing exercise. The confusion is not only in the minds of observers outside France. Within the country, parents have had to accustom themselves to new types of school and to new names; teachers in newly-styled colleges of general education have at times not been sure whether their status was that of the primary school *instituteur* or of the secondary school *professeur*, or whether on some matters such as timetables and curricula they would correspond with Ministry officials responsible for secondary schools while on matters concerned with pay and hours of work they would correspond with an official conversant with primary school conditions; new examinations and forms of examinations have sometimes left pupils wondering what best to study and what prospects would be opened to them by success in the new tests.

The reforms attempt to construct a system that will both do justice to a heritage of enlightenment and democracy and will answer the needs of a modern nation. Among the measures passed within the decade 1959–69, the most important include the Bill submitted in 1957 to the National Assembly by M. Billères, the reforms effected in January 1959 by the Decree of General de Gaulle and M. Berthoin, the law of 31 December 1959 according official status and State subventions to private (Catholic) schools, the administrative reforms carried out in 1960 within the Ministry of National Education, the establishment since 1963 of new institutions of secondary and higher education, and the 1968 legislation affecting the organization of universities.

The relationship of the 1959 legislation to previous drafts will be examined in a later chapter. In outline this was the substance of the law passed by decree and ordinance in January of that year.

1. Children reaching the age of six years would, after 1 January 1959, remain at school until they were aged sixteen years.

2. Obligatory instruction was to include basic skills, the fundamentals of *culture générale* and technical or vocational education. It might be given in public or private schools or even at home.

3. It would comprise three stages: an elementary stage lasting five years, an observation cycle lasting two years and then either a terminal cycle of studies or further general studies or vocational studies.

4. The observation cycle was to be open to those pupils who had 'acquired "the normal elementary instruction" ', and was to be a constituent part of whatever kind of secondary school it served. So far as possible, the curricula of these various cycles were to be similar. A meeting of the teachers, sitting as an orientation council, was to offer advice at the end of the first term of this cycle to the parents of each child.

A main object of this advice was to determine which pupils should start the study of Latin. At the end of the cycle further advice was to be offered. Parents who rejected this second guidance could ask that their children be examined before being allocated to the next course of studies.

5. Pupils who were not even admitted in the first place to an observation cycle might aspire to be transferred two years later into a course of general studies if their teachers recommended such transfer or if examination results justified it.

6. The observation cycle would be staffed by teachers from elementary schools, secondary schools and technical schools. They would receive some special training. But if they taught no classes beyond the statutory leaving age, they would normally rank as *instituteurs* (primary school teachers). Those who were qualified to teach pupils above the age of sixteen, would normally hold a university degree and rank as *professeurs*.

7. Although certain changes in the naming of types of school were decreed, the administrative and financial status of each establishment was to remain unaltered.

The decade 1959–69 was characterized by the reformers' struggle to amend many of these provisions. The period of observation was extended to four years; more teachers operating in the cycle acquired the status of *professeur*; a larger proportion of pupils was admitted to the cycle; and the introduction of Latin was delayed for two years.

A second main piece of legislation enacted in 1959 was the Debré law (31 December 1959) amending the relationship between the State and private (mostly Roman Catholic) schools. This law would, it was hoped, put an end to long-standing educational controversies without imposing complete uniformity. Private schools might retain their existing status. Or the State might take over, or assist schools that requested such intervention. Any assistance offered would be by means of one of two kinds of contract between State and school. By a 'contract of association' the State would bear the expenses of some or all classes where the teaching was in keeping with the State syllabus and with the State's general requirements. The teachers in these classes would be State teachers holding either permanent posts or contractual appointments. In effect, then, the private school would provide State education but retain its own 'specific character and atmosphere'. 'A simple contract' would allow the school to modify timetables and methods more freely, but a limit of nine years (extendable to twelve years) was placed on the duration of such a contract. 1971 was a year of decision for many schools. Difficulties in drawing up or in interpreting contracts were to be referred to conciliation committees of the original departments or of the Ministry; but ideological differences in fact rendered such committees inoperative throughout the decade.

The administration of education

Various forms of legislation and of administrative action were the first of the steps taken in a series which has not yet reached its end. We should note that political decision and its implementation—though motivated by pressures that can be called social or economic, and though not sufficient to satisfy all that reformers demand—were necessary steps, and that especially favourable political circumstances, followed by ten years of stability in which to build new structures, were an important factor in the process of change. Political acts set the process in motion, and the political framework then proved to be one within which Ministers and civil servants could partly redesign the structure of secondary education.

These measures had some effect upon each other. The reforms effected by Decree in January 1959 were inevitably weighed in the balance against the 1957 Bill which the National Assembly had not enacted. Control over the 'observation cycle' instituted by this Decree and over the granting of status to private schools under the law of 31 December 1959 necessitated the creation of new functions within the Ministry of National Education and hastened the partial reform of its internal structure.

Before 1959, the Ministry contained within itself several main branches, each with its own director, administrative services, financial department, inspectorate and sphere of influence. The main branches were those controlling primary education, secondary education, technical education and higher education. The introduction of an observation cycle in which were merged pupils of widely differing abilities for whom a common syllabus was to be devised, and in which teachers of differing qualifications and rank were to be active, led to a partial breakdown of these departmental walls. The appointment of a Director-General of Orientation and School Programmes, the fusion of certain inspectoral functions and the establishment of general service departments (e.g. for personnel and for budgets) are to be viewed as significant developments in the growth of a unified administration.

Technical education

One-third of the young people leaving school take up employment without having received any previous vocational training. For girls, this training is especially lacking. Of those who in 1966 were enrolled in technical and vocational schools and institutions, 560,000 were following short courses in the upper secondary school, and 27,000 were in higher technical courses. It was agreed that the situation was unsatisfactory. The balance between shorter and longer courses was wrong. Outlets for those following the upper school courses were discouragingly inadequate. Curricula and methods still needed to be adapted to the purposes of technical education. Too large a number of authorities (several ministries, private schools and employers) were engaged in technical and vocational training.

A partial solution to the problem of integrating technical educa-

6

tion with general schooling (so that the former should not start too soon and should not be looked on as a separate but lower form of education) was sought in the new comprehensive colleges of secondary education, where different forms of teaching are given in the same institution. Another part of the solution lies in the certificate of vocational studies to which the short upper secondary course leads, and in the technician's *baccalauréat* which crowns the longer school course. The former recognizes studies done in one of three short courses: educational, or commercial, or administrative. The latter recognizes studies done in such fields as mechanical construction, electro-technics, civil engineering, technics of physics or chemistry or biochemistry; and this form of *baccalauréat* leads on of course to higher studies.

Between these two qualifications lies the *certificat d'aptitude professionnelle*, of which several hundred varieties exist. The proliferation of specialities reflects that interest in early specialist qualification which is always in tension with the aims of a more general education.

The repeated effort by reformers to upgrade technical education by raising the number and the status of technical schools and by crowning the various courses with certificates of national worth, was itself crowned in 1966 by the establishment of University Institutes of Technology. These institutes contain departments teaching such studies as electronics, information science, administration of public bodies and of businesses, energetics, physical measurements, chemistry, etc. Entry is by possession of the *baccalauréat* or of an equivalent diploma from a technical *lycée*, or by special examination. Great hopes were pinned on these institutes, but in October 1970 their budget was actually reduced because out of the 45,000 places available in the academic year 1970–1 only 28,000 were actually taken up.

Examinations and orientation

Achievement in the French education system is signalled by the successful passing of an examination and the receipt of the appropriate certificate. The elimination of the examination seems to be impossible. The secondary school entrance is still administered to large groups of children, and a large group of teachers would oppose any attempt to admit pupils from private primary schools into public secondary schools without examination. The certificate of primary studies which, until 1967, marked the end of schooling for those who had never succeeded in entering a secondary course, was then replaced by the *brevet d'enseignement de premier cycle* (*BEPC*) which proved popular with the parents even of pupils who expected to go on to the next three-year cycle of secondary studies. The *baccalauréat* examination which crowns the work of the *lycée* has been subject to confusing modification throughout the decade. In 1962 it was redesigned so that the first part of the examination (which was hitherto sat in two sections in two successive years) was reduced to the function of a trial test. In 1964 it was decided to abolish even this preliminary procedure. At the same time, new papers were introduced to give greater opportunity to pupils wishing to follow technical or geographical or economic studies in their last three years rather than the traditional literacy curricula. This modification resulted in a tendency to specialization which many parents and teachers deplored, and in turn to an adaptation of courses so as to introduce more optional studies. Options and guidance are the alternatives to rigid courses dominated by examinations. Announcing in July 1968 that the study of Latin would be postponed until the third year of secondary school, M. Edgar Faure said: 'Thereafter, secondary schooling is to have a common trunk which unifies the basic subjects. . . . Around this common trunk one can foresee optional branches.' He foresaw too that any given class might be dissolved at times into autonomous groups, each pursuing an optional study at its own level and pace.

The multiplication of courses and examinations makes guidance essential. Proposals for the establishment of a National Office of Information were approved by the Higher Council of National Education in May 1969. These reinforce the development of provisions for continuous guidance, and the Office with its branches in each academic region supplies to parents, pupils and teachers the necessary information about vocational openings, training courses and qualifications. The whole apparatus of national and regional advisory and executive committees is admitted to be cumbersome, and of course the operation depends for its success on how well the class teacher co-operates with the school's medical officer, social worker and vocational counsellor. But despite any clumsiness this is felt to be less arbitrary and less cruel than decisions reached on the basis of examinations alone.

The movement towards the elimination of 'failure' and towards the provision of alternative courses and outlets has its recent parallel in higher education. The creation of University Institutes of Technology in 1966—an entirely new provision which, it was optimistically hoped, would make attractive opportunities available to 250,000 students by 1972—has already been mentioned. Other decrees and orders promulgated in 1966 laid the guidelines for two successive cycles of study in the universities. An existing introductory year of study (*l'année propédeutique*), at the end of which many students failed the qualifying examination for further study, was abolished to make way for an organization based, like the new secondary school courses, on the concept of 'cycles'.

The first cycle offers fundamental training for two years and leads to a university diploma in scientific or literary studies. The second cycle of two years leads either to a licentiate's or to a master's degree (*licence* or *maîtrise*). The former, which recognizes the student's synthesis of knowledge acquired in three years of university study, qualifies the holder for secondary school teaching and for further study. So there are three levels of qualification and the steps between them are less alarming. Holders of the master's degree may proceed to the third cycle, which is designed to train research workers.

These are new structures, but they do not supersede the existing arrangements for the professional training of secondary school teachers (*professeurs*) in regional centres to which access is by competitive examination (*concours*), and for selecting by a further academic *concours* those university graduates who will teach the upper classes of the secondary school and the undergraduates in the universities. This higher qualification (*agrégation*) is acquired by examination in one's academic subject and by its exposition in a model lesson lasting forty-five minutes. Its acquisition entitles the holder to style himself *agrégé*, to be remunerated on a higher scale and to teach fewer hours than those who are not so qualified. The qualification and the procedure have been under attack for some years (see, for example, the journal *Esprit*, June 1969), and M. Louis François, himself an inspector-general in the education

9

service, stated the case for its abolition in these terms (*Cahiers Pédagogiques*, September 1970).

The examination, he said, used to select good teachers in the first half of this century—intelligent dynamic young people who knew how to study, who were enthusiasts for their subject which they knew in some breadth as well as in depth, and who could convey this enthusiasm to a class as well as to a panel of examiners. They passed the examination between the ages of twenty-one and twenty-five, took employment and got married. What they taught in school was a valuable contribution to the general culture that was transmitted to pupils. Now, however, their knowledge is too specialized to have this general cultural value. The candidate is still encouraged to show the depth of his specialist knowledge and to shine for forty-five minutes in front of a class, i.e. to do brilliantly before the class and the examiners what his examiners will subsequently condemn as outmoded: talk while the pupils take notes. Moreover, the standard of scholarship has declined, and even so most of the *agrégés* escape from secondary schooling into higher education if they can. So the schools benefit little. The attraction of the qualification in terms of teaching duties and salary has a harmful effect meanwhile on many candidates for the certificate qualifying them to teach in secondary schools (*certificat d'aptitude professionelle à l'enseignement secondaire —capès*). This also is gained by competitive examination and the syllabus includes a considerable element of professional pedagogical training and study; but those who have declared themselves to be candidates for the higher qualification are excused from certain parts of this training.

Just before he left the Ministry in the summer of 1969, M. Edgar Faure announced his intention of abolishing both these competitive examinations and of introducing new institutions. His successor, M. Olivier Guichard, proved less radical. He announced in October 1970 that new institutes for training secondary school teachers would be set up gradually from 1971 onwards, that the staff of these institutes would be recruited by another *concours*, that the products of the new system would probably enter the schools in 1975 and that the *agrégés* would benefit after 1971 from a year's supervised in-service training, the content of which he did not reveal. Meanwhile *l'agrégation* remains.

M. Faure's other innovations, introduced in the summer and

autumn of 1968 following the student riots, are gradually being implemented. Out of a fairly monolithic *Université* are emerging recognizable, and to some extent autonomous, universities. Into a structure controlled by national officials and professors have intruded the committees of joint control by teachers, students, administrators and technical personnel. And across the barriers of self-sufficient faculties there is some painful growth towards the concept of multi-disciplinary universities and courses of study. All this is far from complete, and in a later chapter we shall look more closely at the legislation within which these mutations may take place.

Democratization: a modern mission

These measures have been presented to the public in France as steps towards the 'democratization of education', and the use of this slogan to express the modern mission of the system gives rise to further debate. For Frenchmen are not agreed as to its meaning. It can mean simply the extension of school into more and more sections of the population; and this is attempted by such measures as raising the minimum school-leaving age to sixteen (with some relaxation of the law in some cases), and by tightening the supervision of attendance. Penalties for unjustified absence from school fall on the truant's parents, whose family allowance may be stopped or who may be fined or imprisoned, and upon adults who admit a child to a public place of entertainment during school hours. More positive encouragement to those families who remain unconvinced of the value of instruction as opposed to wage-earning is offered in the form of transport to school, school meals, supervised homework rooms at school and scholarships. Raising the general level of instruction in any nation is, of course, a slow operation: about half the population of France in 1962 had not studied even to the level of the certificate of primary studies, and this large group of adults must include many parents whose appreciation of extended schooling for their children is less than enthusiastic. Of the young adults now aged between thirty-five and forty, who may be presumed to be the parents of children now passing through the secondary schools, only 7 per cent have qualifications equal to, or higher than, the *baccalauréat*. The fraction of this age-cohort who passed the *baccalauréat* examination in 1966 was approximately one-eighth.

The age of compulsory schooling was extended to sixteen by the reform legislation of 1959, and this measure was to take effect in 1967, so that pupils reaching the age of fourteen in 1967 would stay on in school for two more years. However, the commission preparing the Fifth School Plan (1966–70) could not foresee adequate conditions in which to receive so many extra pupils before 1972. A transitional arrangement has been made for that quarter of the school population which actually would have left school at the age of fourteen (the others staying on voluntarily). This introduces a form of vocational education in which practical training is given by enterprises for about twenty-eight hours a week, and the schools offer twelve hours of education in basic subjects and general culture. In the opinion of those who speak for the organized teachers' unions, this arrangement represents a withdrawal from democratization as a development of the State school system, in particular of its technical education, and a regrettable return to dependence upon employers for the professional training of young prople.

The State, they claim, has failed to provide the necessary conditions for the government's own reforms, and has also failed to meet the educational needs of those who profit little from a highly conceptual, verbal tradition of secondary schooling. Democratization has, then, another meaning: the extension of what schooling offers has to be accompanied by its translation into terms which make it assimilable by a majority of pupils. The practical work done by slow learners in their section of the secondary school does not fulfil this requirement, which is for a pre-apprenticeship education offered in school but preparing for industry, based on school learning but looking for its application to the problems of industry. Without such courses, it is claimed, there remains a serious gap between school and life—i.e. the life of wage-earning in a rapidly developing technical nation—and the school system cannot claim to be adequately democratic. But however improvised and ill prepared these measures may have been, it is possible that they carry within them the seeds of development into a more coherent policy that may in time relate school learning and industrial training more satisfactorily.

Reforms may in time produce fruits; they also reveal the next problems to be solved and in a sense even create them. Thus the abolition of fees for secondary education in 1927, the creation of upper primary schools with syllabuses comparable to those of the first two classes in a *lycée* in 1937, the integration of these schools into the secondary system in 1945 and the constant rise in the number of scholarship holders must all have contributed to the growth of pupil and student numbers that has been called the 'school explosion'.

In part, this increase is clearly due to a rising birth-rate. Each age-cohort is increased from 600,000 children in 1939 to 840,000 in the 1960s. As could be expected, enrolment of pupils in primary schools has risen in similar proportions, but enrolments in various kinds of secondary schools have risen disproportionately fast, and this growth has both alarmed politicians who have had to provide budgets, equipment and teachers, and has given cause for some satisfaction to some politicians who interpret the rise as an aspect of democratization. There is some justification for such an interpretation, since the secondary schools could only have increased their numbers so significantly by both drawing pupils from social classes not hitherto attracted by lengthy studies and delayed earning, and by retaining more pupils for a longer period of schooling until the *baccalauréat* level is reached.

This response to the new social and economic pressures reflects new aspirations and new demands that are being met by the extension of educational facilities to greater numbers of young people. This is reckoned as part of the process of democratization, but although this progress is very satisfactory, it is very far from the equality of chances for the children of different social classes.

Altogether 55 per cent of children of that age were entering secondary-type schools (i.e. those with programmes of study designed to lead on to still higher education), and the target set for expansion is often quoted as 75 per cent. According to forecasts, which as we have seen were not to be fulfilled on time, all the children aged fourteen and fifteen were to be retained in school in the academic year 1968–9, and it was expected that two-thirds of them would stay on beyond the minimum leaving age. As the plans neared fulfilment—and the schools are still far from attracting the majority of children in some social groups and in some geographical regions—the new obstacles emerged more clearly, for a change in the quantity of children being educated means also a change in the nature of the schooling to be offered. So democratization signifies schools in which the mass of children can achieve satisfying growth, and this has tremendous implications for the syllabuses, the teaching methods and the training of teachers.

So far we have been considering the spread of acceptable education to pupils of secondary school age. But there is a more radical interpretation of 'democratization' offered by M. Roger Gal, when he was head of the research department of the Institut Pédagogique National, in an account of his investigations into the problems raised by reform. M. Gal (1965) insisted that the process had to start with the pupils' entry into primary school if the balance of disadvantage which a child brings from his social and cultural background is to be redressed before any selection of courses is made for him at the age of eleven. Children who are gifted or are attentively supported by their parents are successful in primary school; those who need help most fall behind, repeat a year or two, are discouraged and finish up in the 'transition classes' reserved in the secondary school for the weakest 30 per cent of pupils. M. Gal's contention was that only one pupil in two gets through the primary school syllabus at the required rate. Simply accepting more pupils into secondary schools was, he said, no solution. What was needed was a primary schooling that gave pupils time to absorb the fundamentals of reading and of writing, that was sufficiently varied to cater for individual needs and that did not upset the child by passing him on to a new teacher every year. Research into the children's mastery of fundamentals showed this to be so poor that investigators were led to diagnose a much too speedy mechanization of these processes before they had really been understood and absorbed by the young learners. For M. Gal, democratization was a sham unless there was a real rise in the level of school work done by an increasing number of pupils, and the guidance or orientation of pupils into suitable courses was not the assessment of measurable capacities so much as the 'psycho-socio–pedagogical' action that had to compensate for discouraging home conditions.

Another interpretation of democratization is offered by M. Jean Capelle who sees it as the process that guides a young person to the place in society where he will be happiest and most useful. Viewed from another angle the process can be called the maximization of productivity in the educational system. This implies guidance and selection so that the élite can be promoted out of the mass.* The principles on which M. Capelle bases his proposals are four in number: arouse in the young the motivation towards certain vocations; maintain the equal dignity of the choices offered to them; provide a self-regulating mechanism in the system, namely that ambition will be tempered by increased risk; keep alive for all the hope that further advancement is possible.

M. Capelle sees clearly that no simple formula for democratization exists, since plans have to be fitted into the existing social context and educational structures. A further complication is bound to lie in the difficulty of reconciling his three aims. Personal happiness and personal usefulness may or may not coincide in a person's life. And the requirements of an efficient system serving society as a whole may restrict the choices made available to a student. Schools may have a general mission which can be described in normative terms, but its interpretation into more proximate aims uncovers problems of translation into institutional fact that have no straightforward solution. A description of the structures of the French education system and some account of attempts to reshape it will illustrate the difficulties.

The education system: an outline

For children of six to eleven, schooling is offered in primary schools for boys and girls or both, and is organized in three phases: the preparatory course (one year), the elementary course (two years) and the middle course (two years). There is a sense in which the primary system extends beyond these five years. One of the options open to a pupil of eleven or twelve is the college of general education, a four-year course of studies which complements what has already been achieved and was in fact until 1959 called a *cours complémentaire*. This cycle of schooling is given by primary school teachers in establishments administered as primary schools and characterized by a certain pedagogical outlook. It is from this cycle that there have been recruited, by competitive examination, pupils aged fifteen and sixteen who enter the teachers' training

* See *L'Ecole de demain reste à faire*, Presses Universitaires de France, Paris, 1966; published in English in 1967 by Pergamon Press as *Tomorrow's Education, the French Experience* (tr. by W. D. Halls).

school, the *école normale*, to prepare themselves in three years for the *baccalauréat* examination and, in a fourth year, for the teaching profession. The teachers' training schools are also reckoned administratively to be part of the primary system, so the cycle of primary education can for some teachers encompass all their education, even though their professors in the *école normale* are recruited from the secondary corps of teachers.

The primary schools have long enjoyed the confidence of parents, especially in country districts and small towns; and their complementary courses, especially in Paris, win a high reputation. In the countryside the primary school teacher has traditionally been a respected personality playing an important part in the social life of communes and small towns and often occupying the office of mayor's secretary. Since the teacher is often also an electoral agent for a political party, probably to the left of centre, he represents an organized force to be reckoned with even though his personal status in a local community may have diminished since the days when his salary and car were enviable in the neighbourhood. The morale of the corps of primary school teachers is subject to other strains too. The larger annual cohorts of children began to enter the primary schools in 1951, but not until five years later did the *écoles normales* increase their intake of students and in the meantime teachers were recruited from those who were leaving the *lycées* or the first year of the university. These achieved permanency of appointment after three years of teaching. A similar threat to the homogeneity of the primary corps has come from the 'promotion' of those well-qualified teachers who have moved into colleges of general education and have, by length of service or by further training, qualified themselves to be called *professeurs*. And a third disturbing factor has been the gradual extension of State aid to private (mostly Catholic) schools, which is to many teachers an offence against the secular tradition of the national school service.

For many pupils the passage from primary to secondary education, that is to say from class seven up to class six, is a matter of guided transfer; but those whose class record falls below twelve marks out of twenty, or who are transferring from a private school, need to sit an examination. Nevertheless, the school's records of performances in class tests and the teachers' recommendations carry great weight in determining whether a pupil will enter a *lycée* or not; and this decision is a determinant of much that follows in the pupil's career. Class six (*classe de sixième*) in a *lycée* is still the norm to which the classes of other rising types of secondary school aspire to approximate. The classes six, five, four and three (in that order) make up the first cycle of secondary education, and its conclusion is made the occasion for observations and advice offered to parents about the pupil's future by the orientation council. The four years of study are characterized as *culture générale*; they contain no element of professional or vocational training but stress facility in language, in abstract thought and in approaching new problems. In principle, since the autumn of 1969, the former distinction between a classical section and a modern section of class six has been removed. Most pupils follow common studies and are introduced to Latin as part of the French language syllabus studied in class five. Division into classical and modern sections then takes place in class four. Those pupils who, on entry into class six, do not qualify for secondary education proper, enter a 'transition section' whose courses, taught by methods adapted to suit the more modest level of the pupils, complement the groundwork done by the primary school; and after two years the classes are called 'practical' and introduce some technical work.

As institutions the secondary schools vary according to whether they house some or all of these sections. The *lycée* has at least the first two sections, and offers a second cycle of classes for three years beyond the first cycle. The college of general education has the second type of modern section and a cycle of transitional–practical classes, but does not normally take its pupils into a second cycle. The college of secondary education was founded in 1963 because the process of building bridges between these two kinds of school, one of which looked ahead to academic excellence and the universities while the other developed the excellent qualities of the primary school which it so ably complemented, proved too difficult to be an effective form of democratization. This new college contains all the options offered in the first cycle of secondary studies. It is hoped that in such a comprehensive school the passage of pupils from one section to another, should their developing abilities require this, will be facilitated. The colleges of secondary education may be of three types: they may be built as new schools in a new population centre; or they may be developed as more complete forms of already existing colleges of general education which they may in time super-sede throughout the land; or they may operate as semi-autonomous sections of large *lycées*, in which case the second cycle of studies only comes to be regarded as the *lycée* proper.

The colleges of general education which, formerly as *cours complémentaires* capping the primary schools, enjoyed great popular-ity, may be losing favour. It is claimed by some French teachers that some parents even prefer now to send their children to a private school that offers classes up to the *baccalauréat* level, and indeed that some private schools have used their subsidies to build courses and accommodation that are very attractive and rival the State schools. It is of course possible for a school staffed by teachers belonging to a religious teaching order to collect the subsidy for staff salaries, which are then handed over by the teachers according to their vow of poverty, and are used for the general purposes of the institution.

There is no doubt that the colleges of secondary education also, trying as they do to combine within themselves the various tradi-tions and excellences of the *lycée*, the *cours complémentaire* and the senior primary school, are subject to great stress. An official investi-gation into these schools in the Paris region and elsewhere in the provinces showed (*Le Monde*, 8 September 1970, article by Guy Herzlich) that new teaching methods had proved stimulating and successful but that the tripartite structure combining *lycée*, college of general education and transitional classes was still too rigid. Those who taught in the general section especially felt the strain; they were trained in one or two academic subjects but were expected to be versatile general teachers and resented having to be so. More flexible forms of organization involving common classes in many subjects and graded groups in mathematics, French and modern languages were being recommended and tried out in some schools.

The staffing of the *lycées* is by teachers holding a university degree (*licence*) plus a secondary school teacher's certificate (*capès*); and by *agrégés*. To gain one's *licence* a student sits examinations at the end of each of three years. Teachers in a college of general education might hold the diploma in literary or in scientific studies granted at the end of the first two years of study without having completed the full licentiate's course; or they might hold the special certificate designed for those who aim from the outset to occupy a post in that type of school. Teachers in the transitional–practical classes should have received special training; and the college may also call on the specialist but part-time services of *professeurs* from other schools. All these grades of teacher may be found in the colleges of secondary education, and this sets these schools a particularly difficult exercise in staff co-operation.

At the end of the first four-year cycle pupils are guided into one of various forms of a second cycle. Short courses of one or two years lead to vocational certificates and employment. Longer courses of three years are started in one of three sections of the *lycée*: literary, or scientific, or industrial–technical. In the following year these sections fan out into five main streams of study corresponding to the principal divisions of the *baccalauréat* examination. These are:

(*a*) Literary, linguistic and philosophical studies.
(*b*) Economic and social sciences with an introduction to pure and applied mathematics.
(*c*) Mathematics and physical sciences.
(*d*) Natural sciences and applied mathematics.
(*e*) Scientific, industrial and technical studies.

This qualification gives a student right of entry to a university where successive cycles of study lead to a diploma, a *licence*, a master's degree (*maîtrise*) and a doctorate. The more brilliant and ambitious pupils spend two extra years in the post-*baccalauréat* classes of specially designated *lycées* preparing for the competitive examinations that give entry to one or other of the *Grandes Ecoles*. This term *Grandes Ecoles* has never been officially defined. These Great Schools are State colleges linked to various ministries and they train the higher officers for the army, the civil administration, business management, the teaching profession and research work. The schools have no legal link with the universities, and although the question of their integration into the general system of higher education has often been discussed, the university legislation of 1968 left the issue open. Each university may establish its own form of co-operation with such schools as *l'Ecole Polytechnique*, *l'Ecole Nationale des Chartes*, *l'Ecole Nationale Supérieure des Arts et Métiers*, *l'Ecole Pratique des Hautes Etudes*, and with any of the three *Ecoles Normales Supérieures* for the training of secondary school teachers. Admission to one of these three schools means for the

19

student the enjoyment of library and teaching facilities that are better than those available in the overcrowded university faculties, so these specially selected students have a high rate of success in the competition for the extra qualification, *l'agrégation*. Those who gain this distinction teach fewer hours a week than less qualified colleagues in a *lycée*, are paid on a higher salary scale, have special status as teachers of the highest classes and aspire also to teach in a university or in a regional pedagogical centre for training secondary school teachers. The number of *agrégés* that the *Ecoles Normales Supérieures* actually contribute to the manpower of the secondary school system is, however, small compared with the number of those who qualify directly from the universities; and of that small number many subsequently move into higher education.

The differences in status between various grades of the teaching profession are indicated by the following table.

TABLE 1. Salary scales, October 1969

Grade	Salary index figure	Monthly salary in francs
Primary school teacher in training	235	867
Primary school teacher maximum	500	1,717
Head of primary school maximum	560	1,920
Professeur in college of general education maximum	560	1,920
Head of college of general education maximum	605	2,070
Certificated *professeur* beginning of career	340	1,202
Certificated *professeur* maximum	785	2,673
Professeur agrégé beginning of career	390	1,374
Professeur agrégé after three months	430	1,484
Professeur agrégé maximum	1,000	3,391

2

The education system
and attempts to reform it

Dissatisfaction with the system

The organization as a whole still bears the stamp of Napoleon's design. He called it *l'Université*, but it is no longer as unified as the singular noun implies. One section after another has been developed or added or juxtaposed. Thus, for example, primary schools grew ambitiously, and successfully at their upper end, developing complementary courses that offered skills as well as general knowledge, and upper primary classes that transmitted general culture. These remained until 1960 quite parallel to and distinct from the traditional Napoleonic secondary school, the *lycée*. Moreover, the two types of school catered for different social classes: the primary school for those who did not aspire to higher education and professional status; the traditional *lycée* for those who could defer wage-earning and whose intellectual talents demanded the recognition of at least a first university degree—the *baccalauréat*. The *lycées* competed too with the primary schools by extending downwards, making provision for pupils younger than eleven years of age who wanted early attachment to a *lycée* that they would later expect to enter as secondary pupils. At their upper end, the *lycées* developed special classes for those who aspired to achieve, by competitive examination, entry to one of the *Grandes Ecoles* that rank even higher than the normal university faculty.

A similar kind of history accounts for the fact that the integration of technical schools into the general system is still recommended by Frenchmen who contend that this process is far from complete, however unified the system may be made to look on an official diagram. Technical education developed partly in the complementary courses already mentioned, and partly in the practical schools attached to industrial and commercial firms, and partly in schools set up by the Ministry of Commerce at the end of the last century.

French Schools and Colleges—A Simplified Chart

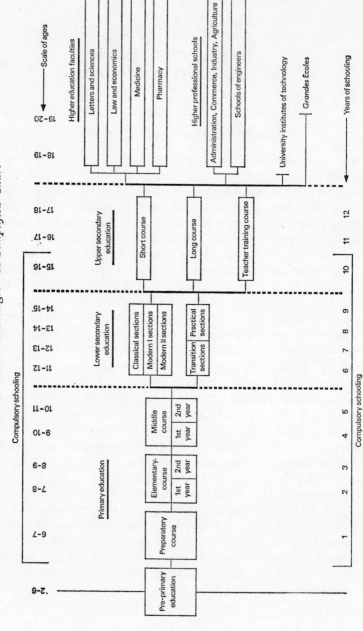

Despite the high prestige of certain schools, especially in Paris, and of engineering colleges, technical education still needs to struggle for respect, budgets and highly qualified teachers. On the other hand, it is more open than the traditional schools to contact with the world of industrial production and of trade. Agricultural education still comes under the Ministry of Agriculture; and various other ministries (e.g. Justice, Defence, Public Works) as well as industrial enterprises operate their own training schemes or even their own institutions of higher education.

The problem of the private sector

The charges laid against the unreformed system were therefore: disunity, social distinction, denigration of technical studies and the

TABLE 2. Numbers of pupils and students in public and private institutions 1965–6

Type of school	Public	Private
Kindergarten and infant classes	1,436,000	256,000
Primary school	4,872,000	842,000
Classical, modern and technical *lycées*	1,184,000	404,000
Public colleges of general education and private complementary courses	759,000	170,000
Colleges of secondary education	96,000	—
Technical schools	337,000	206,000 *
Ecoles normales	36,000	—
Universities and *Grandes Ecoles*	390,000	22,000 †

* Most private technical education is secular not Catholic.

† These students are probably in 'private faculties' offering full-time education of university standard, the students being enrolled for State examinations. In addition there may be about 5,500 students in theological colleges and seminaries.

erection of such barriers between competing systems that a pupil's school career was virtually determined by the decision made with regard to his schooling from the age of eleven years. But these were not the only sources of disunity in this far from monolithic system.

For alongside the public national structure there exist the schools controlled by the Roman Catholic Church. The secular anti-clerical Frenchmen call them 'private' schools. The adherents to the Church call them 'free' schools. Until 1959 aid from State sources to such schools took two main forms. Under the Barangé law of 1951 parents of children in private schools received a small annual grant which the schools' parents' associations were expected to contribute towards teachers' salaries. Under the Marie law of the same year, pupils from private schools are entitled to receive State bursaries. Since 1959, as we have seen, the amount of State aid has been increased and its nature altered, by the grants allowed to schools entering into simple or associative contracts with the State. The table on p. 23 indicates the importance of the private contribution to the nation's educational effort.

Control from the centre

In important respects, however, the State retains controls which ensure a large measure of uniformity. The statutory university alone grants degrees, and as the *baccalauréat* examination, success in which sets the seal on secondary school studies, is technically the first university degree, private *lycées* enter their pupils for the examination and teach the prescribed syllabus for each subject. The Ministry issues from time to time recommendations about methods of teaching. Teachers are advised, visited and assessed by the inspectorate; and though some latitude is admitted with regard to the methods a teacher adopts and the order within which he teaches the items prescribed in the year's syllabus, the pressure to conform and to render a written account of lessons taught is sufficient to ensure more uniformity than could be discerned in the schools of some other nations.

Within the Ministry of National Education are several branches: higher education; pedagogy, schooling and orientation; personnel; equipment and building; social and administrative services; co-operation with other organizations and countries; national libraries. The Minister appoints his directors to each main branch, and his Secretary-General co-ordinates their operation. The Minister is advised by the National Council for Higher Education and Research, which he has certain obligations to consult but whose

24

advice he need not take. This Council is a formidable body, thanks especially to those of its members who represent various teachers' organizations, and it is common practice for a Minister to inform the Council of his proposals or even of his decisions and then to leave his senior civil servants to cope with the ensuing debate. The University Orientation Law of November 1968 required that besides the elected representatives of universities and of other public educational establishments one-third of the membership should be competent lay people, particularly those with knowledge of the nation's economic and social activities. This provision was designed to overcome the isolation of academic organization from the world of industrial production. The Council's duties are: to pave the way for the planning of higher education within the framework of the national plans; to co-ordinate the study programmes and general policies of the universities; and to make proposals with regard to national diplomas and degrees. The Council, like its replicas at the levels of the *académie* (an educational region with university facilities) and of the *département* (the unit of local administrative control) also acts on occasion as an appeal tribunal in matters of professional discipline. Each main pedagogical branch within the Ministry also has its advisory council on which sits an Inspector-General along with regional educational officers and representatives of the appropriate teaching and administrative personnel.

Control is delegated from the Minister to the officials of each of twenty-three *académies*. These are areas of educational control, each having within its boundaries a university or group of universities. At the head of each academy's system of education, acting both as Chancellor of the university and as the Minister's representative in that region is the *recteur*, whom the Minister has appointed. Like the Minister, the *recteur* has his councils and inspectors. His Regional Council for Higher Education and Research co-ordinates the activities and studies of the region's group of universities and gives its opinion on requests for new courses of study and for funds. On the council sit both the elected representatives of the universities and those from other establishments and regional interests. Each university has enjoyed, since 1970, a degree of financial autonomy within general budgetary limits. It is administered by an elected council presided over by a vice-chancellor (*président*) elected for a minimum of two years and a maximum of four years from among the professors. The *recteur* or his representative also sits on this executive council.

The *recteur* has his *inspecteurs d'académie* who represent him in each administrative *département* where, with the Departmental Prefect they administer primary education and inspect secondary schools. The director of a secondary school, even of one of the old prestigious *lycées* which enjoy national status and some financial autonomy (i.e. freedom from local municipal control) is very much an administered as well as an administrative officer. For the offices of the *recteur* cover all the educational services: personnel, budget, accounts, higher education, school planning and building, school curricula, equipment and examinations, social and medical services, inspection, youth service and sport.

A few specialized institutions of higher learning, such as the *Collège de France* and the *Ecole des Chartes*, are administered directly from the Ministry. So also is the corps of inspectors-general who visit and assess specialist teachers in secondary and technical schools. This fact, which distinguishes *professeurs* from *instituteurs* (the latter being supervised by inspectors in the service of a *département*) is an important factor in determining the status of various grades of teacher. Nor do all schools have equal status. *Lycées* and technical *lycées*, whether ancient State foundations or more recently nationalized or still in the ownership of a municipality, are public establishments. So are the new Colleges of Secondary Education. But the vast majority of schools do not have this legal status which entitles them to own land, receive legacies and gifts, carry over some unspent items in an annual budget and enjoy the benefits of legal personality. So the primary sector is again markedly different from the secondary sector; and it is to the former that the colleges of general education belong despite the title of *professeur* acquired by some of their staff.

It is important to realize the long history of thought that supports the concept of the State as a national agent for education. In the eighteenth century La Chalotais, while reserving to the Church all teaching about matters divine, insisted that moral conduct was of concern to the State. In fact this subject (*la morale*) appears in the French schools' timetable. It is usually linked, significantly, with civic instruction. During the French Revolution, Condorcet presented to the Legislative Assembly a plan for a national system of schools. And some of the *Grandes Ecoles* famous for advanced studies, such as *l'Ecole Polytechnique*, *l'Ecole des Arts et Métiers* and *le Conservatoire de Musique*, are proud to date their foundation from the period of the revolutionary Convention (1792–5). This link with the revolutionary past, far from being forgotten, is referred to in a Bill for the reform of education that was presented in the 1950s. Throughout this century reformers have felt it right to claim descendancy from the secular, republican, egalitarian idealism of the Revolution. Viewed in this context, the measures adopted in 1959 hardly seemed adequate, and the succeeding decade did in fact show that they represented only the first attempts to bring flexibility into a rather rigid and hierarchical structure.

The recent history of reform

Let us recall that the reforms decreed by M. Berthoin and President de Gaulle in January 1959 extended the period of compulsory schooling to the pupil's sixteenth birthday, altered the names of several kinds of school without changing their nature and linked the first two years of secondary schooling in an 'observation cycle' controlled by a council of teachers and designed to give guidance to pupils as they moved towards a decision about the length and nature of their subsequent studies. This cycle did not, however, constitute a 'middle school' in any sense, for although M. Berthoin aimed at the 'harmonization of syllabuses' for these two years irrespective of the type of school in which the subject-matter was being taught, the cycle remained clearly a part of each school and shared the school's characteristics. In June 1962 the observation period was extended to four years so that the factor of social determination influencing the performance of pupils in their early years of secondary schooling could be more effectively met. In 1964 the first four years were declared to be 'an observation and orientation cycle', but the cycle was still not made 'autonomous' as a separate middle school would be.

It followed naturally enough that no specialized vocational education could be given before the period of general education had been completed, so technical education was postponed until the fifth year of secondary schooling. Opening a debate in the National

Assembly in 1963, six years after the discussion of the Billères Bill, the Minister presented his proposal for further reform. He defined his goal in secondary education as being 'to substitute for a cleavage founded on social position, on fortune, on geography or simply on chance, a genuine orientation that would put each child, rich or poor, urban or rural, on the track to which his intellectual aptitudes or gifts invite him'. The reforms of 1959 were, he admitted, incomplete; only slightly more than half the pupils in an age-group had in fact been admitted to a truly secondary class; the duration of the observation cycle had been too short and vocational studies had been introduced too soon; and the observation cycle had been functioning in schools that were so distinct in tradition and in staffing that transfer from one school to another had been impeded. The reasons for which a school without partitions had not so far been established were that this idea 'came up against realities, against those institutions, deeply rooted in the tradition of our country, which we call secondary education or primary education with its prolongation into "complementary courses" now styled colleges of general education'. The Minister then announced his intention of setting up twenty experimental multilateral secondary schools—and called it 'the first attempt to make these two forms of schooling really live together and, if I may use the expression, to tame their conduct with regard to each other'. In addition to these twenty schools the Minister proposed to develop a more comprehensive system of schools—not a system of comprehensive schools —so that all pupils would pass from the elementary cycle of education (five years) into a truly secondary cycle. Towns and cities, he said, would retain their *lycées* and their colleges of general education. Rural areas would be served by colleges of education which would not be staffed by specialists each teaching his own subject, because in such areas 'the school population is too restricted to permit the creation of classical and modern *lycée* sections requiring the presence of a large number of *professeurs*'. Small towns and developing urban districts drawing on a population of about ten thousand would have new multilateral (*polyvalent*) colleges of secondary education offering a four-years' course of study. This period was thought of as an 'orientation cycle'.

'All our labels, all our pedagogical traditions are cracking', said the Minister, as the demographic wave broke with its full weight on succeeding classes; but although labels were changed, and the structure cracked, it was not swept away. At the end of 1964 the Minister announced, for example, his dissatisfaction with the working of the *baccalauréat* examination. Each year, he said, of those who presented themselves for part one and part two of the examination (taken in the penultimate and the final years of the *lycée* respectively), 40 per cent failed; and a year later half of those who had passed the second part were rejected by the university on the results of its examination of students at the end of their first academic session. Instead of a sequence of dams to block the flow of students, the Minister wanted a system based on guidance towards one of a variety of further studies. Those whose studies after the first cycle would be 'short' and who would leave school at sixteen would go into industrial, commercial or administrative courses with a vocational purpose, taught practically and concretely. Those pupils following a 'long' course would, on leaving the first cycle, enter a second cycle lasting at the most three years. One examination was now considered sufficient to test the work of these three years; so the first stage of the *baccalauréat* examination was abolished.

Thereafter students could choose between the *Grandes Ecoles*, the various faculties of the universities and the new *instituts universitaires de technologie*. The declared purpose of these new institutes, five of which were opened in 1965 and many more in 1966, is to offer to holders of the *baccalauréat* certificate and to others who pass an entrance examination a choice between branches of higher education, and to prepare these students for supervisory posts. A two-year cycle of study leads to the diploma in technology. Each institute constitutes a unit of teaching and research within a reformed (1970) university structure.

So the principle of organization based, the Minister claimed, on guidance, diversification of options and study cycles was extended from the *lycée* to the universities. In looking forward to a choice of higher education the secondary pupil leaving the first cycle was to opt for a literary stream, a mathematical–scientific stream or a technical stream; and in his next class he was to choose one of five main sections.* The former certificates in technical or commercial studies, taken at the end of this three-year cycle, were upgraded to

* The students' reaction to this 'streamlining', which they felt to be restrictive, was unfavourable; see Chapter 6.

the status of *baccalauréat* and now gave access to the appropriate university faculty or institute.

In the university faculties the first cycle of studies now lasts two years and leads to a university diploma in literary (or scientific) studies. Increasingly, students are receiving recognition for the level of studies reached, instead of being dismissed as having failed to achieve certain fixed degrees. A third year of study for specific certificates leads, among other qualifications, to the teaching *licence*; and this third year together with a fourth year make a second cycle leading to a new degree—the master's degree or *maîtrise*, which in turn is a necessary qualification for those who hope subsequently to acquire by competitive examination the status of *agrégé*. The third cycle of university studies leads to a doctorate and is the preparation required of a research worker.

In outline, then, this is the French response to the pressure of growing numbers and rising aspirations, to the need for trained manpower and to the growing volume of knowledge that must be transmitted. 'And we have not finished', said M. Fouchet, announcing his plans to the National Assembly in May 1965. 'The reform will be a continuous creation around fixed points.'

One of the fixed points is certainly the concept of guidance or orientation. M. Fouchet established an Office of Information and School Orientation, whose functions his successor, M. Peyrefitte, described in February 1967 as being: national, regional and local services to inform parents and teachers of the openings available for young people both in employment and in forms of further education; advisory service to teachers and pupils in the schools; the assembly and training of teams of advisers or counsellors including school doctors, educational psychologists and teachers who will have equipped themselves by experience and special training. M. Peyrefitte stated categorically that the basic principle of the reform was orientation, by which he meant the guidance of pupils into secondary courses according to the pupils' tastes and aptitudes.

But there is no single clear primary aim. In the 1966 debate M. Pompidou had stressed the need to adapt secondary education to the modern world, and to raise both the number and the quality of passes in the *baccalauréat* examination. The intention to make the system more democratic has not displaced its more traditional function: the selection of the élite. Critics of the reforms so far carried out asserted both that the new structure was still not fully democratic—since the pupils who are to study the classics are chosen early in the first year of secondary schooling and the other pupils are kept in sections that do not meet, so that there is no heterogeneous grouping of abilities and interest—and that many students reached the universities whose subsequent academic performance did not justify their entry. For some critics the next development was a truly common, undifferentiated, comprehensive *classe de sixième*.* For others, the urgent need is to promote lively intellects as rapidly as possible and therefore to run the secondary schools in three distinct streams; the bright, the average and the slow. Others again would recommend some mixing of the bright and the 'above average', or some mobility permitting pupils to be in the fast group for one subject and in a slower group for another subject. As the number of pupils following secondary courses increases, the reconciliation of democratization and selection is felt to be increasingly difficult.

The third aim mentioned by M. Peyrefitte, namely modernization of the system, may not be so clearly at variance with other intentions. By modernization is meant the redesigning of structures and programmes so as to increase the relevance of what is taught to post-school life and to the country's economy. Diversification of paths open to pupils at the end of the first four-year cycle fits well with the development of orientation to guide them in their choice of occupation or study. There is, however, no guarantee that a pupil's personal inclination will lead him into the technology or the science that manpower economists would recommend. Another indication that relevance or usefulness to the economy has been accepted as an aim was contained in the law of 3 December 1966 on Orientation and Curriculum, concerning vocational, technical and further education for young people and adults. Its declared purposes were: to establish a system of post-school education that would help workers to respond to the economic needs of the country; and to stimulate and co-ordinate the activities of public authorities and private enterprises in such matters as apprenticeship and retraining. The law was presented as another link in the chain of reforms and

* This was achieved in the summer of 1968 after the students' revolt; see below.

Structure of Education After the Reform, 1966

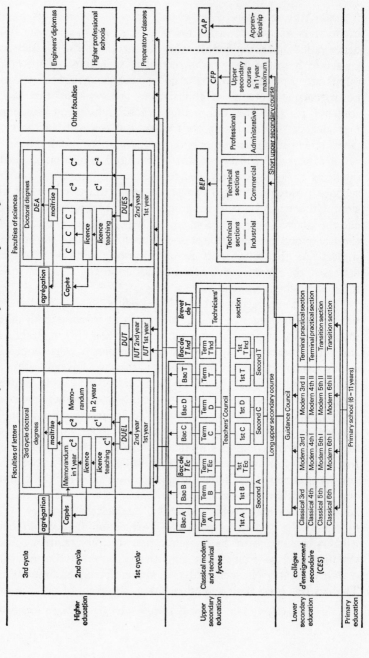

Abbreviations

Bac de T Ec	baccalauréat de technicien économique (technician's baccalauréat in economics)
Bac de T Ind	baccalauréat de technicien industriel (industrial technician's baccalauréat)
BEP	brevet d'enseignement professionel (vocational education diploma)
C	certificat
CAP	certificat d'aptitude professionelle (vocational aptitude certificate)
Capès	certificat d'aptitude professionelle à l'enseignement secondaire (certificate of aptitude for teaching in secondary education)
CFP	certificat de formation professionelle (vocational training certificate)
CES	collège d'enseignement secondaire
DEA	diplôme d'études approfondies (diploma of advanced studies)
DUEL	diplôme universitaire d'études littéraires
DUES	diplôme universitaire d'études scientifiques
DUT	diplôme universitaire de technologie
IUT	Institut Universitaire de Technologie
Term	terminal class

as an attempt to establish some equilibrium between training resources, employment needs and further education.

Recurrent difficulties

These analyses of existing structures and of the need for change all contain references which testify to enduring elements in the problem. The first is the restricting nature of the heritage. So much that has been handed down was excellent in its day but is now a limitation: the priority of subjects, the respect for the *lycée*, the selection of the academically bright, the scholarly delivery by the master on his dais, the discipline, the buildings and the formation of the corps of teachers. This is of course not the only characteristic of tradition which can be a source of inspiration and invention; but for the French reformers the weight of inheritance is felt mostly as an encumbrance. Yet an established nation with an educational service dating back for centuries cannot redesign its institutions on a blank sheet of paper; and this is the second main fact to be borne in mind. There is bound to be an unequal development of institutions.

A third recurrent theme is the discrepancy between a pedagogical ideal—often referred to by French educationists as *culture générale*—and its translation into practice. Admiration of the well-made rather than the well-filled head is expected from all politicians and educationists, who then go on in speeches and writings to deplore the stuffing of these heads with insane amounts of knowledge prescribed or at least invited by the syllabuses which pupils have to cover in order to equip themselves for examinations. Thus the traditional ideal advocated by the essayist Montaigne is distorted by the practices handed down from the early nineteenth century. Greater consistency between theory and practice is among the aims of the present reformers.

In many respects the action taken by politicians has fallen short of the hope cherished by reformers, but even so the political thought of the Ministers has sometimes proved to be too optimistically in advance of the practices in schools. Berthoin's hope that the harmonization of the syllabus followed in different secondary schools would be possible and would prove to be the key to reform was not fulfilled. Neither was his expectation that a sufficient number of bridges to ensure 'democratization' could be thrown between various kinds of secondary school. It is doubtful whether even the colleges of secondary education will build them. Expectations are frequently excessive.

In order to discover how adequate the analysis of forces, faults and remedies proved to be during more than a decade of reforming activity, we shall have to examine the proposals and the obstacles they met. Besides such elements as the status of various groups of teachers, the social framework into which reforms have to fit—or which they have to reshape if they have revolutionary power—may well include the status of church schools, the degree of unanimity in the body politic, the beliefs held about the functions of schools and about the nature of the *culture générale* and the humanism they impart, and the strength of the conviction with which the fundamental principles of the Republic are held. And even if frustrating conditions or groups are known to exist, the reformers may have underestimated their intractability.

3

The Ministry of National Education

The administrative obstacle

The Minister of National Education is, of course, a politician as well as an administrator. He has to navigate in certain currents of power. These stem from the students' unions and groups, from the leftist views of many teachers and from their professional conservatism, from the restraints almost habitually imposed by the Minister of Finance and from the various teachers' unions. The National Assembly has been consulted less than the Higher Council for Education and has tended to be impotent rather than potent among these forces. A very revealing debate, but not one which produced any legislation, took place in 1957 on a bill presented by M. Billères. The Reform of 1959 was passed by Decree. Between that date and 1968, Ministers reported occasionally to the National Assembly and took some note of comment on their own proposals, but no great interest was displayed until the events of May–June 1968 made imperative some legislation for the reform of higher education. Occasionally a Minister has the will or the imagination to leave his mark on the educational system despite the politicians' tendency to move in and out of government from one ministry to another.

Such a Minister was Jules Ferry, for example, who in 1881 and 1882 established primary education for the people and insisted that it should be free, secular and obligatory. Another such was the brilliant young Jean Zay who, between 1936 and 1939, extended the period of compulsory schooling to the age of fourteen years, introduced an apprentice scheme for all young people entering industry, established welfare services for students, set up experimental 'orientation classes' and tried, without success, to win acceptance for the concept of *l'école unique*, the single comprehensive school offering a unified service to the nation's children. And although M. Faure's period of office was much shorter than these two great Ministers enjoyed, he may well be remembered in future for his

work from May 1968 until May 1969 when he calmed student
wrath and introduced, in a liberal spirit of understanding, reforms
which some of his parliamentary colleagues felt to be too concessive.
Commenting on his replacement of the intellectual, scholarly and
much admired M. Faure by a successor having no direct links with
the university, M. Pompidou explained (just after his election as
President of the Republic in June 1969) that an occasional outsider
brought in to consolidate the work of innovation could make a useful
contribution to reform.

For many years problems relating to the Ministry's internal organization have been recognized. Certain parts of the organism are, so
to speak, missing. These are chiefly the post-secondary schools of
engineering, military science, commerce, administration and mining
that are operated by other ministries. Entry to these establishments
of higher education is greatly prized; they are referred to as the Great
Schools (*Grandes Ecoles*); and they have only a loose connection
with the *Université* in the Napoleonic sense. Another problem is the
disparate nature of those sections that do form part of the Ministry.
There are operational sections such as the National Centre for
Scientific Research, the University Bureau of Statistics and the
National Pedagogical Institute. There is a Secretariat for Youth and
Sport. There are advisory offices supplying the Secretary-General
with information about planning, budgets and statistics. There are
common logistic services, such as welfare, school equipment and
personnel. And there are branches whose directors control higher
education or school education and orientation. Much of the effort
of the last few years has been designed to detach the logistic services
from each of several branches concerned with a sector of the school
system, to unify these sectors and to amalgamate their organs of
service.

The problems derived naturally from the historical growth of the
main teaching branches. These grew, as we have seen, parallel and
in competition, each branch overlapping with another and each
equipped with the advisory council and with the budgetary and
personnel services it needed to operate its own realm. The inspectors
too had specialized functions and tried not to trespass on each
other's territory. And the teachers were, and still are, distinguished
by title, salary, competence, training and status. So the internal
structure of the Ministry reflected, in its divisions, the socially

37

divisive structures of the school system, offering to pupils quite recognizably differing ranges of opportunity. Just as it was difficult to break down partitions between types of schools, to create harmonized syllabuses and to get head teachers to agree to the concept of easy transfer of pupils between classes (this agreement was never won, and for quite good educational reasons); so it was difficult to break down walls between the school branches organized in the Ministry.

Tentative changes, 1960–4

Some reorganization of the inspectorate took place in 1960 and 1961 when a combined corps of inspectors-general was made responsible to the Director-General of Organization and School Programmes. This corps was given special responsibility for the operation known as 'drawing the school map', i.e. taking decisions about the closure, extension or building of schools in response to movements of population and industry. Their function obviously transcended the boundaries of ministerial departments. Supervision of the new orientation cycle which, it will be recalled, might be located in schools of different types, was also entrusted to an Inspector-General in each academic district. This kind of redistribution of functions across boundaries pointed the way towards a more 'horizontal' organization of the Ministry and to the elimination of some of the vertical partitions separating branches.

The relationship between external reforms and administrative adjustments has several times been demonstrated. In 1944, for example, a co-ordinating post of Director-General of Education was created hopefully; and it was abolished eighteen months later when the National Assembly failed to vote on, and therefore to implement, the far-reaching Langevin–Wallon Plan that would have established *l'école unique*. Another attempt was made in 1960, which as a reform corresponded in its aims and in its incompleteness with the measures decreed by M. Berthoin in the previous year. This time the Director-General of Organization and School Programmes tried to combine the administration of primary, secondary and technical schools. But so long as the three sectors remained separate in many respects and not fully merged even in the observation cycle, this new administrative branch was bound to suffer more internal strains; and in fact it was broken up and the functions were re-allocated in 1962. More definitive reforms took place in 1964.

More definitive reforms, 1964–8

In February 1964 the Council of Ministers approved measures that elucidated the functions of a new secretariat-general (actually established by a decree dated October 1963) and that redesigned the structure of the Ministry.

In addition to the Minister's own cabinet of personal secretaries and advisers, there was introduced the office of Secretary-General responsible under the Minister for co-ordinating the main branches and functional services, and for directing the corps of inspectors-general. The instruments of control put at the disposal of the Secretary-General included a bureau of statistics, a bureau for budgetary and financial planning, and a department responsible for drawing up the school and university development plans. This last department maps the location of new schools and faculties, and does so in relation to the overall development forecasts of the National Plan.

Under the Secretary-General were established seven main branches or directorates:

1. The Director-General of pedagogy, schools and orientation, with responsibility for general, technical and special education, for syllabuses, teaching methods and examinations, for the guidance services and for collecting data that will determine the future appearance of the school map.

2. The Director of Higher Education, or more exactly since December 1964, of Higher Studies in the plural. He is responsible for the teaching, the personnel and the institutions of higher learning, and in this respect still resembles one of the former all-embracing 'vertical' branches.

3. The Director of Teaching Personnel in Schools is obviously in control of a service department with a 'horizontal' function.

4. So also is the Director of School, University and Sports Equipment.

5. The Director of Administrative Services looks after the welfare of non-teaching staff, and also the allocation of bursaries.

39

Two other directors ensure co-operation with overseas territories and international agencies, and the service of national, university and public libraries.

Concurrently with the regrouping of functions in the Ministry was enacted also some modification of the various councils attached to different services. The *Conseil de l'Education Nationale* was reconstituted to consist of: five representatives of the private sector; twenty-five members nominated from the administration; twenty-five members from other ministries, from parents' associations, from persons having special competence, from students' associations and from trade unions; twenty-five members elected by the teachers. The councils attached to the teaching services were reduced to three in number, notably by the coalescence of the three councils concerned with primary, secondary and technical schools into one Council for General and Technical Education.

The official text introducing these reforms set them in the context of social and economic pressures to which all such adjustments are said to be a response, and claimed that the changes necessitated in their turn, tighter administrative control.

The needs of the economy, which is impoverished if aptitudes are misjudged or badly employed; the technical needs which require of all, innovators or executives, a continuous adaptability; and finally the social demands of far greater equality—all these imperatives together necessitated a radical reform of the basic structures of our education system.

The creation, then the remodelled versions of the Directorate-General of School Organization and Programmes, which embraced—firstly by type of schooling then later by type of function—the services responsible for operating the schools, were the reflection of these needs.

The structures thus modified, plus the new discussions of the task, quickly revealed a new necessity: that of a closer administrative co-ordination exercised under the direct authority of the Minister.

The paragraph which concluded the official announcement of these changes repeated the need for unity and introduced also an interpretation in different terms, namely those of pedagogical reform and the development of the orientation services. Students of education will be aware that measures can be interpreted at different levels and will want to consider to what extent these interpretations support or modify each other.

In conclusion, it will be remembered that this new organization has as its object, on the one hand, to endow the very large and complex ministerial apparatus with the organs essential for 'piloting'—regrouping the means (budget), organizing forecasts (plan), knowledge (statistics), and unifying authority—and that it tends on the other hand to constitute groups of services around simple functional concepts (problems of pedagogy, or of personnel, or of equipment). At the same time it throws into relief, as far as various types of school are concerned, the importance that must be attributed in future to both pedagogical reforms and the organization of school guidance services.

Three years later the Minister established an Office of Information and School Orientation to serve parents and teachers, and he promised a commission to study problems and methods of pedagogy. Pointing away from the structure of the Ministry to the more sensitive areas of school work and guidance, which are the teachers' responsibility, the indications seemed to suggest that the Ministry thought it had completed its contribution to the new design of an education service and that the next steps in the chain of reform would be taken elsewhere.

It is of course true that enormous problems remain to be solved; the professional training of the enormous numbers of teachers who have not received any professional training; the in-service training of those who sense that their knowledge and methods are outmoded but can do little about it; the whole question of pedagogical method; the overburdening of pupils and the excessive discussions of syllabuses; the meaning or orientation. But it could also be true that if the Ministry were less concerned with control, administration and unification and were better designed to promote reflection and policy-making in the councils, the drafting of plans in its offices as opposed to the successful handling of each emergency, and research that would convince teachers of its applicability, then the Ministry could be an instrument of reform rather than an overworked, ponderous machine.

However hard Ministers and a few brilliant directors may have tried to reform their administration in the rue de Grenelle, the feeling persists that it is not a dynamic element in the system. G. Dreyfus, reporting in 1967 to the *Assises Générales* of the Gaullist political *Union pour la Nouvelle République*, found that the Ministry was largely in the hands of former *professeurs* (because the secondary teachers' unions liked it that way), and he suggested that a few top administrators from a different stable would not come amiss. The graduates of the National School of Administration were too rarely attracted to so ingrown a service. In a decade of computers and electronic equipment, thousands of clerks were still employed making out pay-slips. The commissions contributing data for the national plan were too far removed from the regions and operated clumsily. Delegation of responsibilities and powers to the *recteurs d'académie* would help if they too could be equipped with adequate machinery and staff. The inspectors-general, whose tasks are to advise the Minister and to assess teachers, had little inter-disciplinary expertise but more influence than any progressive head teacher. Their influence tended to be conservative in the key operations of introducing a new syllabus or in drawing up new teaching instructions.

There can be little doubt that in this sphere, as in so many others, all changes effected so far have represented a compromise and must be held to be incomplete and impermanent. They must be viewed, along with those which will develop as the 1968 law on higher education is implemented, in the light of recurrent criticism of the central administration. Brilliant men associated with the Ministry—Langevin, Le Gorgeu, Monod, Capelle—or with the *Institut Pédagogique National*, or with the Caen Colloquium, have proposed reforms, some of which have been incorporated into legislation after which it has taken up to ten years to put the measures into effect. The raising of the school-leaving age, decreed in 1959, was only partially implemented in 1968. 'Harmonization of syllabuses' in the first cycle of secondary schooling, declared by M. Berthoin in 1959 to be the key to reform, was not achieved until in 1968 M. Faure abolished the teaching of Latin to the brightest stream of eleven-year-old pupils in the *lycées*. The interests of various professional groups, well represented on the Ministry's councils, have to be respected with the result that the councils can act as a brake but, having little power of initiative and no authority, cannot provide that dynamic impulse which some critics say the Ministry lacks. Where does the energy for change and growth come from ? From the immediate demographic and economic pressures, which impel administrators to magnificent efforts that produce each September a fairly adequate increase in staff and accommodation for the rising numbers. But this annual *tour de force* itself inhibits reflection about long-term policy, and reduces the concept of administration to that of making a response rather than taking an initiative. Nor has anyone outside the Ministry any authority for the latter. It remains to be seen whether the new experimental 'units of higher education' near Paris and the more autonomous universities in the provinces will acquire authority to administer themselves in the sense of making policy. Without such an infusion of power and local authority the system must remain 'under-administered', in that overworked civil servants in the Ministry, although numerous, are too few, are ill-equipped and are too preoccupied with the immediate.

For students and teachers the reforms already effected have produced unwelcome complications. The difficulties met by university students in organizing their studies were intensified by the abrupt application of M. Fouchet's new system of cycles. And the redesigning of the Ministry itself along more 'vertical' lines meant that a head teacher who previously corresponded with only one branch (primary or technical or secondary) now may have to write to one branch in relation to his own salary and career, and with other branches about staff, equipment or a syllabus. Participation by parents, students and pupils in such an administration via the new school and university councils may prove frustrating to those who hope for a say in the policy of autonomous institutions—those that want to budget for development over a period of years (not just annually), to organize themselves regionally, to control their own size (nothing has been said in the 1968 law about selection), and that look to the Ministry for the dynamic of political decisions about democratization, orientation, selection, financial resources and relationships with the employers who use the system's products.

Presenting his 'orientation law' to the National Assembly in October 1968, M. Edgar Faure spoke of 'administration' as if it were synonymous with participation in councils:

That the university should be administered by those who work
in it, by those who profess in it, by those who learn in it . . .
that does not mean the dismemberment of the public authority;
on the contrary, it is guaranteeing under the best possible
conditions the service of a society which made us its guardians.

It was in reply to this sort of interpretation that Professor Alfred
Grosser (writing in *Le Monde*) asked: 'If a teacher is competent to
administer just because he has been elected, what is the point of the
management schools of industrial enterprises, and what is the use of
the National School of Administration?' An adequate answer to
Professor Grosser would require a Ministry organized as a national
enterprise, staffed by trained administrators and equipped with
modern aids for long-term planning.

The changes reported in this chapter were made in response to
recent legislation and to some of the pressures that produced the
legislation. The principle of French administration remained unaffected; decision was made at the centre in the capital; the authority
by which decisions were imposed was reflected in duties delegated
to the *académie* and to the *département*; and the nation was kept
unified and stable by the impartiality and uniformity of an administered educational process that could truly be called a system.
Whether this administration really responded adequately to the
needs of teachers for initiative, new methods, flexibility of approach,
freedom to use local resources, develop environmental studies,
could be questionable and the question was violently put in 1968
when student dissatisfaction erupted. It was put again in the plans
for regional reform which President de Gaulle adumbrated, but,
having opted not to take the senators into his confidence in a matter
which touched them closely, failed to carry by referendum in 1969.
What was in question was in fact the nature of the State and the
style of its governors, and these are not really remote from the
problem of creating an educational ministry that will promote
democratization and give encouragement to new relationships in the
classroom.

Equilibrium, system and unity are not universally held to be the
prime functions of the State whose citizens, especially the younger
ones, are clamouring for change, creative freedom and diversity.
Dissatisfaction is felt, too, about the pace at which the vision is

implemented of a system that would pass beyond impartiality and the justice of controlled examinations to the concept of discrimination in favour of partially disinherited groups and the provision of conditions that enable growth. Some of the frustration felt by those who have vision but do not realize it is laid at the door of bureaucracy, and in particular of the Ministry. The image of organization as a mould or matrix is increasingly discarded and resented; and in its place are preferred structural arrangements that do not ossify and that do not inhibit the processes of change. A Ministry whose departments appear also to institutionalize certain socioeconomic inequalities can expect to be attacked, not only on the grounds of inadequate internal organization but also as a political arm of government. Certainly such considerations were expressed by discontented students who, in 1968, were aware that in rejecting the official arrangement of living quarters, examinations, lectures, courses and certificates, they were also rejecting the government whose Ministry was too rigidly organized in the name of stability. The generous vision that for decades had inspired reformers among French educationists had to do with the organization of a more just society in which educational services would not only be open to those who could profit from them but would compensate in some measure for lack of stimulation and richness in young people's environment. Adjustments within the Ministry have hardly improved the consumer's view of a bureaucracy. The anti-bureaucratic slogans which proliferated in 1968 also expressed the citizens' sense of powerlessness, and their removal at some distance from the locus of decision-making. Few structures existed for facilitating discussion and participation. As a result of violent revolt these were quickly designed and put into operation within a year. And the limitations put upon the Ministry of National Education by the Ministry of Finance were suddenly removed, so that land was acquired, buildings were taken over, new universities were erected and legislation was enthusiastically passed by the National Assembly. But the dynamic had come from outside the Ministry. Imaginative response came from the Minister. And a year later a new period of consolidation and stability was proclaimed by the incoming President.

PART TWO

The politics of education

4

General issues

There is much agreement among the main political parties of France in their analyses of the need for reform and of the obstacles in its way. Even a moderate conservative supporter of President de Gaulle would concede the importance of the Langevin–Wallon proposals, the inhibiting influence of the *agrégés* in the National Assembly of the Fourth Republic and the narrowly partisan policies of various professional associations. All parties would agree that Parliament had effected no significant reforms before 1959 despite the recognition of immense demographic pressures as the birth-rate grew, economic pressure as the agricultural sector shrank and employment in tertiary services expanded, and social pressures as people demanded more education for their children. All parties were convinced too of the need for democratization of the hierarchical educational systems. Independent statistical analysis had shown that the social class structure of the country was reflected inversely in the student population, the university and the *Grandes Ecoles*; in 1963 three-quarters of the students at the *Ecole Polytechnique* were the sons of managers or executives, and so were half the students in nearly all the other *Grandes Ecoles*. It was known too that the rural population of France was handicapped. All parties saw the importance of technical education for the country, and recommended its expansion. All looked forward to the eventual transfer of agricultural education from the Ministry of Agriculture to the Ministry of National Education. The whole system was recognized too as inefficient in its production of qualified manpower; of 65,000 students entering higher education in 1963 only 25,000 were expected to receive their diploma or degree three years later. And all recommended an increase in the financial resources allocated from the national revenue to education.

Until the turbulent events of May and June 1968, the combination of parties supporting Gaullist policies (*Union Démocratique pour la cinquième République; Union pour la Nouvelle République;*

49

Union Démocratique du Travail) could congratulate themselves on their rapid expansion of the education service, and they claimed to have fallen only slightly short of the targets set by the Plan, to have doubled in ten years the number of teachers in higher education, to have kept 75 per cent of the fourteen to sixteen-year-old pupils in full-time education, to have opened access to university for 60 per cent of students coming from 'modest' backgrounds; to have created new institutions such as the colleges of secondary education and the university institutes of technology and new university degrees. In a report to the 1967 general conference of the UNR–UDT, M. François Dreyfus (a member of the party's central committee and a university lecturer) conceded the great shortfall in the training of engineers, technicians, scientists and doctors and the probable over-production of graduates from the faculties of arts and law. He wondered whether the university could be made more efficient too, so that the proportion of admitted students who emerge with a qualification might be '80 per cent rather than 25 per cent or even less'. He admitted that a university had other important purposes besides meeting the nation's need for manpower, but warned against 'encyclopaedism, one of the most serious tares in our system of education. The system bears its fruit: it kills for everyone any taste for reading and for culture; France is among the developed nations one of those in which there is least reading and least interest in the theatre, in museums and in music.' Dreyfus went on to urge the building of more colleges of secondary education, the development of real orientation, the rehabilitation of technical education by the expansion of autonomous technical *lycées* as opposed to technical sections in general *lycées* and the inspiration of the whole system by a new concept of modern humanism. He recognized too the need for a new pedagogy, a new professional training and a reform of higher education.

So it was not immobility that characterized the thought of the moderates or even the conservatives in the Gaullist parties. But to their opponents, the amount of movement achieved was inadequate. The annual trick of fitting everyone somehow into school was no longer convincing, according to a statement by the *Parti Socialiste Unifié* (the small rather intellectualist party which encouraged militant students in their 1968 revolt and which helped to transform anti-Vietnam War groups in *lycées* into very active *comités d'action lycéens*). The PSU admitted the fact of an annual increase in the educational budget but asserted that the increase was not so impressive if one took into account rising costs and rising number of pupils, and that anyway there was an increasing gap between the demand for equipment (buildings, furniture and manpower) and the supply. It attacked the interpretation of 'prolonged schooling to 16' which permits pupils to leave school and enter vocational training sections (*sections d'education professionnelle*) in industry, as being a further cession of technical education to the private sector and a dangerous splitting of future technicians into two groups: the mass of those trained on the job in industry and the élite of those taught in technical *lycées* and institutes. The PSU also deplored the divisions and rivalries still existing in the colleges of secondary education, and the criteria of orientation which it alleged were those of adaptation to the mentality of the teaching staff, tending to reinforce the social pressures that already selected pupils too soon for school success or failure.

Radical-socialist manifestos issued in 1967 concurred with this analysis, stressing the need to start reform in the primary schools if socio-cultural handicaps were to be overcome, and the need to organize a really common core of institutions in the first four years of the secondary schools. The radical-socialists did not share the PSU belief in participation by students and pupils, but they did object to the 'utilitarian' view of education ascribed by them to the right-wing parties, and of course to the upgrading of private education by the bursaries, grants and subventions that had received statutory approval between 1951 and 1960.

The Communist Party produced in February 1967 a book setting forth its proposals for reform in education.* It condemned all Gaullist reforms as mere sorting or shunting operations, and demanded the establishment of a common school up to the age of fifteen. The allocation by the government of one-sixth of the budget to education was derided as merely the achievement of an aim set by Jules Ferry in the eighteen-nineties, whereas a modern nation should raise the fraction to one-fourth.

> The Communist Party insists on the re-establishment of strict respect for secularity within the framework of a nationalized system of education and of its tripartite control by the

* *L'Ecole et la Nation*, no. 156.

representatives of the State, the teachers, and the parents of pupils. Of course at the level of higher education the students themselves are admitted to joint control.

Full-time education until the age of eighteen was set as a target, with a much larger place demanded for technical studies. The social classes of the nation were, it was claimed, reflected in inverse proportions in the universities. A general programme of social measures was needed to help pupils to overcome social, cultural and geographical handicaps. And the general condemnation of the schools for their lack of adaptation to modern conditions was expressed by this quotation from the Langevin–Wallon report of twenty years previously:

The structure of the education system must be adapted to the social structures. For half a century the educational structure has not been modified. The social structure on the other hand has undergone rapid evolution and fundamental transformations. Mechanisation, the use of new sources of energy, the development of the means of transport and communication, industrial concentration, the growth of production, the massive entry of women into economic life, the spread of elementary instruction have profoundly altered the condition of life and social organization. The rapidity and extent of economic progress which had necessitated in 1880 the spread of elementary schooling among the working masses, now sets the problem of recruiting an increasing number of executives and technicians. The bourgeoisie, called by heredity to hold posts of responsibility and management can no longer do so by itself. The new needs of the modern economy make necessary a recasting of our education which, with its present structure, is no longer adapted to social and economic conditions.

This maladjustment of education to the present state of society shows itself in the absence or inadequacy of contacts between the schools of all levels and life. Primary, secondary and higher studies are too often on the fringe of reality. The school seems to be a closed environment, impermeable to the experiences of the world. The divorce between schooling and life is accentuated by the permanence of our educational institutions within a society undergoing accelerated evolution. This divorce strips the school system of its educational character. A reform is urgently needed to remedy this lack in the education of the producer and of the citizen, and to give to everyone a civic, social and human upbringing.

Remaining on the fringe of life, the schools have not profited from scientific progress. Empiricism and tradition dictate their methods whereas a new pedagogy based on the educational sciences ought to inspire and renew their practices.

Moreover, at all levels the schools ignore in the pupil the future citizen. They do not attach sufficient importance to the scientific and objective explanation of economic and social facts, to the methodical cultivation of the critical spirit, to the active apprenticeship of energy, liberty and responsibility. Now this training of youth in citizenship is one of the fundamental duties of a democratic State and it is up to the public educational system to carry out this duty.

The document then condemns the system for its inefficiency quoting ministerial statistics that record this backwardness of pupils in the last class of the primary school in 1962–3: one year behind—33·4 per cent; two years behind—13·5 per cent; three years behind—4·8 per cent.

A later number of the same monthly publication from the Communist Party* expressed at least one grievance felt by all those who opposed the style of government by President de Gaulle and a subordinate Parliament. The National Assembly, debating education in May 1967, 'spoke, but did not vote; discussed, criticized and proposed, but did not sanction'. This inefficacy of Parliament, and the powerlessness of politicians while government was carried on by the President and his Ministers (many of whom were former servants of the State, not elected representatives of the people) was in the following year held by some commentators to have contributed towards the explosion of the university's anger. The journal repeated the party's adherence to the Langevin–Wallon Plan and condemned the government's postponement of the higher leaving age. This delay was due, they claimed, to the fact that 'the global figures calculated by the experts having been reduced by the government by about 40%, the authors of the Fifth Plan had had to give up the full application of prolonged schooling before 1970.' The

* *L'Ecole et la Nation*, no. 161, September 1967.

part-time education linked with industrial training that M. Peyre-fitte proposed in its place was of course condemned by the party as the early surrender of children to employers.

There might be some justification for the hesitation felt by opposition parties with regard to the government's illiberal intentions. M. Dreyfus had, in a report submitted to the UNR–UDT for its conference in 1963, proposed that calculations of future manpower should be taken seriously and that 100,000 to 120,000 pupils should be admitted each year to State *lycées*, and the rest should be 'obligatorily orientated' into technical *lycées* or some technical education. The guidance of pupils into an appropriate course of studies would, he argued in 1963, be done in the light of pupils' capacities, parents' desires and also national needs. The decisions of the Orientation Council would be binding. Four years later he admitted that colleges of secondary education did not exist in sufficient numbers, that the continued existence of the four-year cycle of studies in the *lycées* invalidated much of the reform these colleges were meant to inaugurate and that 'orientation at the end of the cycle consists in retaining in the *lycée* the main body of pupils who however could or ought to have been differently guided.' Guidance worked badly, he claimed, because the Orientation Councils regarded technical studies as a less worthy course than classical or modern studies.

He argued also for restricted entry to higher education, for chaplaincies to be attached to schools wherever the parents requested them, for faculties of Theology in other universities besides Strasbourg and for a regrouping of village schools (including Catholic parochial schools) so as to permit more rational distribution of rural schools consisting of at least three classes. For the political left-wing and for the radical-socialists, such proposals raise important questions about parents' rights, students' rights, about the status of the Catholic Church in education, about the legitimacy of taking any account at all of parochial schools when planning a secular State service and about the neutral nature of the *Université*. Just how difficult such proposals would be to put into effect if the National Assembly regained its former importance as an institution of government, or to get accepted in the country at large even if not debated in the Assembly, may be judged by the following two accounts of parliamentary procedure in 1957 (*Projet de loi Billères*) and 1959 (*Loi Debré*).

5

Political constraints: two case studies

Repeatedly in the fifteen years of struggle for reform that preceded the legislation of 1969, the dilemma of politicians has been made manifest. A Minister's case for change has to be related to some principles. If he is to have the support of a political party, then he probably has to base his case upon a recognizable ideology acceptable to a large group of representatives. An ideology tends to elevate a question from the status of a local problem susceptible to pragmatic solution, to the level of a dramatic issue. The perspective of ideology opens up a vision of significant battle, of crucial victory or defeat, of clear distinction between right and wrong, of loyalty to the cause, of association with the heroes, martyrs and prophets of the party's history and of responsibility for the countless unborn whose future is seen to be at stake. The conflict in France between Catholicism and secularism is bedevilled by angels, as it were; both sides have a doctrine and a hierarchy for which adherents still conduct propaganda in the ecclesiastical sense. Organization for battle is not easily adapted to the business of pragmatic reform. Its rigidity can be said to act as an obstacle to agreement; and ideology to act as a restraint upon the movement to reform. Those who feel themselves to be engaged in a significant cause will be strongly energized; they will also be intransigent.

The Billères Bill, 1957

The political ideology of the largest Party in the Chamber of Deputies in 1957 was Marxism–Leninism which was viewed by the Catholic Right as a rival system of thought comparable to a competing religion. In fact, various forms of communism do have their heroes, legends, charismatic leaders, hymns of praise and specially revered places. In a country where doctrines compete and have within memory fought, the concept of a secular State which holds power on behalf of all citizens and against any single rival institution, such as a

55

dominant church, was welcomed by liberally minded Catholics who were relieved to think that the Church was thus freed from functions it should not try to perform. But for many Catholics the secular State was a hostile power; and for many secularists too it was seen as a defence against ecclesiastical control of temporal matters. This latter view was strongly held by the Radical-Socialist Party and by the adherents of Marxism–Leninism. 'Secularism' was an ambiguous term, not yet a formula for national unity.

Hostilities had continued in France from the inception of the Third Republic in 1871, especially in the period between 1882 and 1905 when the Catholic teaching congregations were disbanded and the separation of Church and State was effected. Anti-clericalism was a principal characteristic of the Radical-Socialist Party, and this group constituted an interestingly floating centre in the French political spectrum, for while it voted with the left wing on all matters touching the Church and the schools, its members mostly held moderately right-wing views on other issues. So a left-wing government could count on a fair amount of Radical-Socialist support for the promotion of secular education but not for other socialist measures. And a conservative government could count on their support so long as it did not raise the 'schools question' in the Chamber of Deputies. In 1951 the bill to make monetary allowances to the parents of children in church schools was enacted only by the defection of thirteen Radical-Socialists from the Party's traditional position. In 1956 this law (named after its proposer, Barangé) survived a proposal to abrogate it by only nine votes, and the issue produced impermanent groups of dissidents in nearly all the Parties. In 1957 the Socialist Government which was prosecuting war in Algeria and could not afford to alienate the right wing by proposing measures at home which had long been advocated by left-wing educationists. So the Billères Bill, debated as an exercise in analysis and illumination, was not brought to a vote. And in May of the following year the need to settle the war and to restore national unity at home was so pressing that General de Gaulle was asked to take over government and was accorded emergency powers.

The debate itself shed light but did not generate power, and this fact in itself says something about the dynamics of reform. We have to look elsewhere for the original pressures to change. Nevertheless, various politicians were anxious to claim credit for parts of the bill and to assert their status as representatives of various respectable national traditions. Thus the communist speaker claimed to be heir to the educational thought of the eighteenth-century Encyclo-paedist Condorcet; the moderate centre representative defended the standards of the secondary schools against any invasion and dilution by primary school teachers who would be staffing the middle schools; the Radical-Socialists praised the idea of democratization combined with the selection of an élite; and the Catholic Deputies defended the concept of freedom, meaning the right of church schools to receive public funds. Humanist and socialist and moderate speakers supported the *tronc commun*. These were all recognized as 'political' issues, proper for argument based on ideology. And the idea that the problems of educational organization have to do with govern-ment was accepted. So too was the obvious but frequently over-looked fact that applied government depended on adequate finance.

A compromise position—that most problems could be solved logically without massive intervention by central government—was stigmatized as an anti-revolutionary posture, contrary that is to the principles of 1789, to the concept of a single indivisible Republic and opposed even to the centralizing activity of both the Bourbon monarchs and the Emperor Napoleon. This is a particularly interest-ing characteristic of French political thought because the urge to-wards decentralization was not apparent in 1957, and did not in fact gather any power in educational matters until ten years later. The idea that both political wings shared a doctrine of power that was itself a restraint upon some kinds of reform scarcely could have occurred to the French Deputies by whom the State had been viewed hitherto as an engine of power supplying the thrust for progress.

Other issues were deemed to be hardly political or purely 'educa-tional'. Parents, for example, were mentioned by a Radical-Socialist only to defend their exclusive 'rights' against any incursion by coun-selling teachers into the parental preserve of 'guidance'. No men-tion was made of parents' rights to participate in the councils or the administration of schools. That, too, lay dormant for a decade. And other questions which were mentioned but not explored by Deputies included school transport (necessary if rural areas were not to remain disadvantaged), school terms and holidays (the organ-ization of which was to be challenged by a group of citizens ten years later), the overloading of the syllabuses (frequently subject to pruning and also constantly acquiring new elements), the training of teachers and the shortage of scientists. It was apparent that politicians saw their sphere of activity as the structure of the system and the provision of finance, and that they were less qualified or less willing to say much about the internal operations of the system. Yet the recurrent problem of when to introduce Latin into the curriculum of the secondary school could not be overlooked. The traditionalists defended its early introduction so that a long, slow process of impregnation and of mental discipline might begin and might set the tone for other subjects. For Latin was a 'subject', a body of academic knowledge, a training, a meeting ground for the young mind and the scholar's wisdom, a link with an imperial past, a mark of the old liberal culture not defiled by modern utilitarianism. The defence of Latin became symbolic and politically important.

The limitation upon movement towards reform indicates that there are other restraints upon politicians than the strength of a political opposition. It was clearly demonstrated in the order-in-council and decrees signed by General de Gaulle and his Minister of Education, M. Berthoin, in January 1959. Politically, the General still had the full powers granted to him in May 1958, for the new National Assembly had not yet met. Yet the reforms he decreed were not in themselves very far-reaching. Their significance lay rather in the fact that they started a movement which gathered momentum throughout the decade.

M. Berthoin ordered an extension of compulsory schooling by raising the leaving age to sixteen. This measure was meant to come into effect in 1967. He rejected the idea of a 'middle school' and proposed instead a two-year period of observation and guidance for pupils entering secondary education. This was a dilution both of the middle school concept and of the hope to offer 'secondary education for all' since not all pupils would be allowed to enter the observation cycles. Some pupils would continue their primary studies under *instituteurs* in classes still designated as part of the primary school system. The observation cycles were established in various kinds of school—secondary, technical and also those primary schools which offered the much-appreciated 'complementary courses'. What these observation cycles had in common was not their status or the salary grade or designation of their teachers, or their buildings; the unity of the cycles was to develop thanks to 'harmonization of the syllabuses'.

In effect this meant the gradual approximation of the syllabus in these observation classes to the traditional syllabus of the *lycée*—with the exception that children were still to be graded at the end of the first term so that those who showed promise could start Latin without further delay. Special training was decreed for teachers working in the observation cycle; but this common preparation and work was not to alter their separate status under different branches of the Ministry. The preservation of Latin as a subject of special worth was also a recognition of teachers' susceptibilities. And the location of the cycle in different schools was a defence of the prestigious *lycées* and *collèges* against the threatened flood of pupils of secondary school age which was itself both a major pressure for reform and a stimulus to defensive reaction. M. Berthoin also promised measures to upgrade technical education and did initiate a series of moves to provide technical courses in *lycées techniques*, and their final examinations were ranked as equivalent to the *baccalauréat*. But ten years later the relative status of technical schools was still held to be unsatisfactory by those who worked in them. The limitation in this case was the traditional prestige of non-technical studies which continued to attract students who then went on to study in unwieldy numbers at the university faculties of Arts and Law.

The politicians—both President and Ministers—took limited action in 1957 and 1959, and the limits were set in the two cases we have outlined by differing forms of restraint: overt political opposition as visible in the National Assembly, and latent opposition that might be awakened among supporters who would not want to see the established institutions shaken by demographic and social pressures. Despite their restricted nature, however, the measures decreed in January 1959 were important for they contained the seeds of such potentially upsetting practices as an embryonic common trunk of studies, co-operation between teachers of different status, the opening of secondary education to nearly all pupils and the creation of new institutions for technical education. A third case to be studied was the legislation passed at the end of the year 1959 by a majority of Deputies but in defiance of a radical republican tradition. To this we now turn.

There can be no doubt that the status of private schools became the subject of debate once more because of two main factors: their economic base was crumbling away, and their power in the National

Assembly suddenly increased in 1959. Their status always had been largely determined by political forces.

The revolution of 1848 which brought the republican Carnot to the leadership of the Constituent Assembly of the Second Republic encouraged him to write a famous letter to primary school teachers.

> May our 36,000 *instituteurs* rise in response to my appeal and make themselves straight away the rebuilders of public instruction among our rural population. May my voice reach them even in our furthest villages! I ask them to contribute their share towards the founding of our Republic . . . New men, that is what France calls for. A revolution must not only renew its institutions, it must renew men. One changes tools when one changes work. It is a fundamental principle of politics.

But the Legislative Assembly that succeeded his Constituent Assembly brought into power a majority of the more conservative *Parti de l'Ordre*. It rejected Carnot's secular education bill and passed in its place the Falloux law of 1850. This law recognized the inspectoral rights of the clergy in primary schools, the validity of a teaching certificate granted by a minister or priest, the right of every commune to establish private schools, and of women in teaching orders to teach without qualification other than their letter of obedience. And the law granted to the general council of each *département* the right to close down its normal school for training teachers.

This law was the result of a political compromise which associated the order-loving but anti-clerical bourgeoisie with the clerical but anti-republican party. Such an association was only possible under stress, and the pressure was in fact the threat that both perceived from the working-class revolutionaries of 1848. The influence of Carnot's fervent *instituteurs* had to be kept in check by that of the local priests. The law worked. By 1882 there were five times as many private primary schools as in 1848. The attack on the radically minded *écoles normales* took place ninety years later when the Vichy Government of 1940 suppressed them. It also inaugurated a policy of subsidies for denominational schools. And in 1959, support for a policy of subvention had its political significance too, for it reduced the influence of those many teachers and academics who had showed little enthusiasm for General de Gaulle's return to power on 13 May 1958. The trade union opposition too, which had voted against de Gaulle in his referendum seeking legitimization of his authority, joined the National Committee of Secular Action. Eleven years later, opposition in another referendum brought about his retirement; that part of the opposition's programme which refers to schools still awaited, in 1970, the parliamentary majority which will undo the measures passed in 1951 and 1959.

In a sense, the quarrel is pointless. It has little to do with the real needs of contemporary France. It refers to an issue about which students themselves do not feel strongly, for belief or unbelief are not labels they attach to themselves or to their schools. This diversion of energy and investment into the wrong developments has acted as a restraint upon the more significant reforms that should have been undertaken in that decade. The Association of Parents of Pupils in Lycées (APEL), in supporting these subsidies, could claim that the private schools were doing a public service. The Association was also diverting limited resources from a public service that needed to expand. The governments that gave attention to allowances and subsidies were annually caught short of school places and teachers. And the coalition of those parents with those supporters of private schools formed a front of indifference or even hostility to the schools of the majority that catered for the 'badly brought up' children who threatened to submerge the more 'cultured' *lycées*. So the process of democratization was held up while the needs of minorities were answered.

In 1951 a member of the MRP had referred to the Barangé law as 'the breach through which the flood will pass'. The fear that there is still more to come by way of Catholic claims—especially from Brittany—has kept the secular opposition alive. As we have seen, it is also a political opposition waiting its time for counter-measures. The choice to subsidize was a political one. It was a defeat for the opposition rather than an act of national reconciliation. It perpetuated the practice of making educational issues depend upon parliamentary majorities, and so pointed forward to another reversal of policy when the complexion of the majority changes. Meanwhile, the construction of a truly national education system sufficiently autonomous—i.e. free of immediate government direction—to develop in response to its own needs was held up. But the pressure from teachers, students and parents to share control in the councils of schools and universities was building up to a point of explosion.

The Debré law, 1959

A second piece of legislation produced in 1959 was called the Debré law, after the Prime Minister whose majority enacted it, and it dealt with the relationship between the State and the private schools. This had long been one of the most divisive issues in French politics, and the settlement enacted in December 1959 may still depend for its continuance on a right-wing majority. The issue is a particularly instructive one to examine, since it introduced a pressing financial problem into an already embittered national debate.

The Constitution is ambiguous and often open to conflicting interpretations as M. Debré admitted to the National Assembly when, in July 1959, he set up a Commission under the chairmanship of M. Lapie to examine the problem and propose solutions. Article 2 of the Constitution states that 'France is a secular Republic. It ensures equality before the law for all its citizens irrespective of origin, race or religion. It respects all beliefs.' On the other hand the preamble to the Constitution recalls the Rights of Man as defined in 1789, and among them figures the freedom of education. Both principles were recognized to be essential for national unity.

Past practice was inconsistent. A law of 1886 forbade any subsidy to private schools from public bodies. But those schools which asked for it could receive the special grant allowed under the Barangé law of 1951, irrespective of whether the school was public or private. The grant amounted to 3,900 francs a year for each regular pupil, and in 1958 the private schools thus received a total of 5,000 million francs (i.e. 50 million new post-1959 francs) to be allocated to teachers' salaries. This grant was helpful but barely allowed the salaries of teachers in private schools to rise as fast as those of their colleagues in the public service.

Another inconsistency derived from the Falloux law of 1850, which had authorized the State, the departments and the communes to grant to private secondary schools a subsidy not exceeding one-tenth of the school's expenditure. Eight private secondary schools thus figured annually on the State budget. There was, moreover, no legal text forbidding official support for private higher education.

And technical education had benefited since 1919 (Astier law) from State subsidies and later, from 1925 onwards, from the proceeds of an apprenticeship tax levied on those firms which did not themselves operate training schemes for apprentices. Subsidy is the rule rather than the exception in the technical sector of education and a further source of official funds is of course the bursaries accorded to meritorious pupils from primary schools, whether they are entering a public or a private secondary school.

In 1958 the private sector was by no means inconsiderable. Of 7 million primary pupils, about 1 million (15·4 per cent) were in private schools; of 1·1 million secondary pupils, 440,000 (40 per cent); and of 580,000 technical pupils, 260,000 (44·7 per cent), though in this last sector only 18·2 per cent were in Catholic technical schools. The attendance at private schools was not distributed evenly throughout the country. More than a quarter were in the region of Brittany; and four other departments accounted for another quarter of the pupils. And to complicate the position, three departments of Alsace-Lorraine enjoy a special status based on a concordat whereby the public school is often a confessional school and the denominational teachers are public servants.

Some data were, the commission found, not available. Despite the Ministry's planning and locating of schools in the operation known as the drawing of the *carte scolaire*, the commission was unable to get information enabling it to assess the degree to which public and private schools actually competed with each other in villages or towns. In the absence of these data no conclusion could be reached with regard to the allegations of certain witnesses that the two sectors interfered harmfully with each other.

The will to unity that had characterized secular and Catholic citizens in 1944 had been gradually eroded. A commission chaired by M. André Philip in the winter of 1944–5 had reached unanimous if limited agreement: the term 'public service' would be reserved for the education given by the State; no member of the commission disputed the freedom of education; nor had the idea of a State monopoly been found acceptable. There was hope at that time that secularism would cease to be a position for battle, and that the Church might give up certain forms of spiritual imperialism. Both groups of citizens looked forward to a general national agreement, though the secularists wanted only 'neutral' schools to be accepted as national while the Catholics wanted confessional schools to be accepted and subject to normal inspection.

A second commission was set up in 1950 under M. Paul Boncour, but the secular groups refused to co-operate with it and it had come to no conclusions before the elections of 1951 rendered it obsolete. The commission did, however, stress that the State could not just prolong the existing conditions. Much greater budgets would be needed if premises were to be built and teachers trained for the rising cohorts of pupils. And as that would take time, the State could not afford to ignore the resources in buildings and manpower represented by the private contribution to education.

Although the Boncour Commission's work was largely nullified by intervening elections, it did manage to propose the outlines of a solution which was to be exploited nine years later. These indicated possible degrees of integration. A private school whose buildings, equipment and teachers were taken over would be fully integrated, even if the boarding accommodation remained separate and denominational. Or the State might employ only the teachers and might, as it were, rent the buildings from a private association. Or the State might accept responsibility for financing certain classes or perhaps only certain teachers—excluding, for example, the 6,000 priests and 25,000 members of religious orders who were teaching.

The disposition of affiliations in the 1951 Assembly led to new claims for financial aid and to an aggravation of the quarrel. Two laws were passed which applied equally to State and to private schools and accorded grants to both. The Barangé law made a capitation grant of 1,300 francs per child per term, to be used for the buildings budget of State schools and for the salaries budget of private schools. Defenders of the secular schools objected to this indirect way of dealing with a financial problem that was enormous and could not be solved by such petty measures. They assumed that the grant could only be temporary and that it would not outlast the transient political coalition. Defenders of the private sector presumed that this was a temporary expedient and that a comprehensive solution of their problems would soon follow. The Marie law made bursaries available which alleviated some family hardships but contributed nothing to the national policy. It was in an atmosphere of growing hostility and of hardening positions that the Lapie Commission was set to work in 1959.

Somewhat to their surprise, Deputies in the National Assembly that met early in 1959 discovered that two-thirds of them belonged to the Parliamentary Association for Free Schools which had been promoted by the Catholic Study Secretariat for the Defence of Free Education. Legislation that was not just provisional had been awaited for fifteen years. Demographic pressure on the schools was mounting. Despite the Barangé law, Catholic teachers were not well paid and the number of highly qualified staff was small. Only 45 per cent of teachers in private schools had a qualification equivalent to the university *licence*; they amounted to 8,750 teachers and of these only 291 were *agrégés*. The opportunity afforded by a majority in favour of aid to private schools was seized by right-wing Deputies, and the Prime Minister was forced to submit legislation. No sooner had he announced his intention of doing so than the secular pressure group, the National Committee for Secular Action, protested vigorously. M. Debré appointed the Lapie Commission to hear witness and recommend legislation.

The outlines of the dispute were clear enough. The principle of 'freedom of education' was disputed only by those who wanted to 'nationalize' the entire educational resources of the nation, and in the opinion of the Commission that was 'impossible in the present constitutional, psychological and economic circumstances'. So both sides had to be heard and, so far as possible, satisfied.

The Church maintained that the Constitution recognized in effect that natural and divine law which conferred on parents the right and the duty to bring up their children. In practice this means the free choice of an educational environment, i.e. of a school in which instruction is given, for both intellect and faith should be awakened in the same institution. The fact that 800,000 families had chosen private schools had, it was agreed, virtually established 'a private service of general interest', and had created an educational capital that was now imperilled. Fees and grants together no longer sufficed to meet the cost of maintaining these schools. So the private sector was asking for further aid and would prefer that it be given to some intermediary organ between the State and the family or the teacher or the school; for the chain of schools constituted a general service or system and should not be considered individually.

The defenders of the opposite thesis built their case on the principle of State secularism which, they argued, excluded the possibility of channelling public money into confessional schools. They denied that the 'freedom of education' implied any right to ask the State to subsidize schools that would compete with the public system. Nothing should be done to obscure the fact that the secular State school was national and open to all, and that nobody's opinions would be offended in it. The national schools would accommodate rationalist, agnostic, Catholic, Protestant, Jew or Muslim. To favour any denominational school system would open the door to segregation, and if the public schools were deprived of their Catholic pupils the schools might become less liberal in outlook and the nation's groups less tolerant of each other. And at a moment when the public system was short of buildings, and of manpower, all available public money should be allocated to public schools. To direct resources from the public sector was deliberately to prevent it from meeting the enormous need. The great majority of French teachers, secular and Catholic, it was contended, supported this view, and many were said to hold the opinion that admitting the permanency of a private sector was tantamount to setting up against the national *Université* a hostile *Université* which would be denominational linked with an international order and directed by a foreign sovereign.

It was quickly apparent to the commissioners that a return to this Jacobin position was politically impossible, and that any concessions to the private sector could only be made if the duty of the State to control education was recognized. So the question of inspection and supervision arose. Hitherto, supervision of private schools had been nominal and concerned itself only with morality, hygiene, the salubrity of buildings and the regular attendance of pupils. All those who claimed further subsidies also recognized that this would imply inspection and extended supervision. But the secular witnesses wanted it to include the right to veto textbooks that cast any slight upon the Republic or upon the principles of the Revolution (both of which, it was contended, received hostile treatment in books used by Catholics in Brittany). And the Study Secretariat for the Defence of Free Education wanted it to be understood that while the quality and efficiency of their education might properly be inspected, no supervision should interfere with that characteristic of the free schools which had determined the choice of so many families. It was a characteristic of a spiritual nature. So how could a secular inspector be competent to pass judgment on it? Nor could the right of Catholic head teachers to choose their own staff be subject to State control. The commissioners themselves made clear what they meant when they acknowledged the right of the State to exercise certain super-vision. By financial control they meant only an assurance from in-spectors that any State aid was in fact used to raise the salaries of teachers. By administrative control they meant checking the qualifi-cations of teachers. By pedagogic control they meant that each school would be open to normal inspection by the appropriate branch of the Ministry's inspectorate, and this might mean that, while in-spectors could not impose any choice of textbooks, they might veto specific books.

The commission came to the conclusion that no simple system of subsidy to private schools would be tolerated by the defenders of secularism, and that a practical compromise lay in various degrees of subsidy towards teachers' salaries. This would permit contracts between various groups of teachers and mobility within the national teaching service, and it would necessitate contact between State and ecclesiastical authorities. From such personal contact the commission hoped there would grow mutual respect. The degrees of support proposed were four in number:

1. The State could offer to any private school that requested it a complete change of status from private to public. The property would pass to the local authority and those teachers who were properly qualified would become State employees.

2. A contract might be made whereby a section of the school would be taken over by the State (for example, the primary classes attached to a *lycée*); or the teachers might be taken into the national service; or the State might put some of the teachers at the disposal of a private school. The commissioners were not agreed among them-selves whether all these options should be offered, and whether certain schools might also be allowed to borrow money at a low rate of interest for capital development.

3. An intermediate stage of relationship between the State and pri-vate schools might be made by an agreement that would not be so far-reaching nor so final as a contract. By such an agreement the State might help to pay the salaries of some or all the teachers, but without integrating them into the corps of public servants. The offer

of such an agreement should remain open only for a limited time during which school authorities could make up their minds whether to be linked to the State or not.

4. If not, then the fourth option would be complete independence with no aid.

The government's legislation based on the commission's recommendations was debated in an atmosphere of crisis. The stipulation in Article 1 of the bill that 'teaching was to be given in total respect for the freedom of conscience' roused Catholics to a defence of the committed character of their schools, and a right-wing revolt against the government was only averted because President de Gaulle made the vote a matter of confidence and threatened to dissolve the Assembly if his government was defeated. (The bill was passed into law by 427 votes against 71, with 18 abstentions; and the country realized with some shock that a new style of government had prevailed.) The secularists were offended by wording which allowed the teaching given in private schools to retain its particular character. The Minister of Education, himself a socialist, objected to the fact that instruction would not be neutral and he resigned. So did half of the Supreme Council for Education, claiming that they had not been consulted, as they ought to have been, on such an important measure. The National Council for Secular Action called on its supporters to boycott all local conciliation commissions that might be set up to discuss which form of contract could be accorded to each private school. And the Movement for Free Schools urged its faithful to press for the growth of the truly pluralist education system.

The issue is bound to be active and divisive as long as decisions have to be taken about the continuation of aid under the Barangé law and about the prolongation of those contracts that were supposed in the first place to be interim measures. In the opinion of some observers the system of contracts is becoming an acceptable institution. Most claim that discontent continues to rumble and will become vociferous again when a secular majority is returned to the National Assembly. Meantime, how has the Debré law of 31 December 1959 been used? How many of the less restricting 'simple contracts' were entered into, as distinct from the more integrating 'contracts of association'? Figures published by the Study Secretariat for the Freedom of Education claimed that:

from 1960 to 1 May 1964, for 12,000 primary classes and *cours complémentaires*, 10,441 simple contracts and 147 contracts of association were agreed;

in secondary education (classical and modern) for 1,500 establishments, 509 simple contracts and 304 contracts of association have been signed;

in technical education, for 1,200 establishments, 176 simple contracts and 92 contracts of association have been accepted.

Altogether, out of about 14,700 private classes or establishments, there have been requested 12,800 simple contracts and 680 contracts of association.

If from establishments we pass on to teachers, we note that on 1 May 1964, out of 78,000 private teachers 52,000 had their salaries paid by the State.

All this was achieved, it was claimed, without any loss of freedom. Many of these teachers would however be requested to get, within three years, the qualifications that would give them permanent status on the State's classification scale. A decree dated 12 April 1965 actually opened the way for teachers in private institutions to have access to the competitive State examinations for such qualifications as *l'agrégation, le certificat d'aptitude au professorat de l'enseignement secondaire* and *le certificat d'aptitude au professorat de l'enseignement technique*. Two of the main teachers' unions objected to this facility, declaring that under the law these private institutions kept their *caractère propre*, and that the undertaking to be at the disposal of the Minister to teach in one of these (private) institutions was not comparable to the traditional undertaking given by a secular *agrégé* or *capésien* to serve in the public educational system.

In the year 1965, the expenditure on salaries paid to teachers in private schools under the Debré law was by far the largest of the subsidies to private educational establishments:

Legal Sanction:	Loi Barangé (allowances)	Loi Marie (bursaries)	Loi Astier (apprenticeship subsidies)	Loi Debré
Sum in millions of New Francs:	50·7	66·7	2·4	1,035·8

To this was added 66·4 million paid to private agricultural schools benefiting under a further law passed on 2 August 1960. State participation in private education was, then, sizeable and growing.

The opponents of this growth were preparing themselves in 1967 and the early months of 1968 for massive demonstrations in favour of secular education. Looking forward to the period between 1969 and 1972 when the Debré law must either be suspended or prolonged, the CNAL (Comité National d'Action Laïque) was conducting a campaign against the duplication of schools and the bishops' increasing insistence that they should be represented on commissions drawing up recommendations with regard to the *carte scolaire*. The CNAL recognized that so many teachers could not brusquely be deprived of their livelihood, but asserted also that the existence of two competing systems could not be allowed to continue. They proposed therefore that, as a first step towards a single, secular, national system of education, must be the progressive integration of all those teachers and establishments who had accepted public funds. For this, a new majority in the National Assembly would be a necessary condition.

Whether elections held under fairly normal circumstances would have reflected the growing boredom of the population with Gaullist rule cannot be known. The issue set before the electorate in June 1968 as a result of the students' revolt was presented as a choice between the forces of violent revolution and those of republican order. The massive Gaullist majority returned to the National Assembly by the alarmed voters had probably confirmed the trend of the decade towards State support for private schools and assured the prolongation of recent legislation for that purpose, while the Comité National d'Action Laïque claims that the hesitations of the population as a whole with regard to these developments is proved by the fact that the conciliation committees have never functioned. Dispute may well take place over the interpretation of the *Loi d'orientation de l'enseignement supérieur* (November 1968), Article 5 of which permits the newly redesigned universities to enter into agreements with other public or private establishments for joint co-operation or formal association. The Catholic theological faculties may want to develop such links; and although the granting of degrees remains a State monopoly they may want examiners to take into account the Catholic tutors' assessment of candidates' work done prior to examination. Such assessment is now recommended as part of university procedure. It seems a rational and progressive measure, but it has to be read in the light of its possible interpretation in a nation whose philosophies are not yet reconciled.

It is apparent that 'reform by finance' is not a unifying formula. The offer of more State aid to education has proved to be a bone of contention as well as a nourishing element. This is not to deny that reforms may require increased Education Budgets, but in the circumstances outlined in this chapter, the competition for money exacerbated relationships between various groups in society more noticeably than it drew together men of goodwill.

6

Politics and the University

A structure and its problems

The University of Paris consisted, until 1969, of five main faculties: law and economic sciences, medicine, natural sciences, letters and human sciences, pharmacy; to which were added in 1964 the science faculty at Orsay and the faculty of letters at Nanterre. These served some 125,000 students. In law, the University and its faculties enjoyed 'personal' rights and financial 'autonomy', but these did not guarantee initiative or power of corporate action. It is true that the University appointed its own professors and assistants; and the constitutional guarantees that protect the University from some unacademic pressures also assured to the professor some freedom from interference in the design and delivery of his lectures, and to the corps of examiners the independence necessary to uphold standards. As Chairman of the University Council, a university *recteur* did not exert a powerful control over its faculties and their professors. He did not ensure co-ordination in the total enterprise. But as the regional representative of the administration he was, and to some extent still is, a channel through which the Ministries of Higher Education and of Finance exert their discouragingly detailed and limiting financial control. The weight given to financial control as opposed to the planned equipment, and staffing of an expanding session must be reckoned to be a political phenomenon, for it is a decision about the allocation of national resources. The University of Paris feels the discomfort of control and of parsimony more than do the provincial universities because of the congestion in the capital of a centripetal intelligentsia. The city of Paris itself offers excellent technical schools. The prestigious *lycées* in Paris offer two-year courses that prepare post-*baccalauréat* candidates for the entrance examinations to the *Grandes Ecoles* or, if the candidates fail, make it easy for them, thanks to excellent teaching by the élite of *professeurs agrégés*, to pass the university examinations. Students find lodgings or hostels more easily in Paris. Many specialist courses and much research can only be pursued in Paris. And even some of the professors teaching in provincial universities prefer to live in Paris and to commute to their lecture amphitheatre for a few days each week. Despite the creation of new university centres and research facilities elsewhere, the Paris region continues to draw population from the provinces.

From the point of view of reformers, the university as a whole seemed ridden with obstacles. The apparatus of laws, decrees and orders that controlled its administration, its programmes of work and even its teaching methods, was hard to set in motion. 'The university machine is badly equipped for adaptation to fluctuations in demand and to the evolution of research techniques, since any reform requires the setting in motion of a cumbersome procedure at national level', wrote M. Marcel Merle (1964). Other obstacles designated by him were 'the dictatorship of accountancy' resulting in near-paralysis; the impossibility of creating a policy for a University controlled anonymously in the Ministry; the insistence on uniformity throughout the country as a sort of egalitarianism which leads to the duplication of institutions in one region after another instead of to diversification of courses and of combinations of courses; the complexity of higher education as new institutes, new schools, new examinations were created by other Ministries and public authorities trying to escape from the 'sclerosis of university administration'. Proposals for reform, urged at that time, included: the creation of a Ministry of Higher Education so that long-term policy could be thought out at government level; the separation of the functions of *recteur* and of *inspecteur d'académic* in the university regions, so that the latter only would represent the public authorities, while the former would confine his attention to the work expected of the elected president of the University Council; the abolition of annual accounting, and the granting of university budgets under a few main heads; the transfer of control over the faculties and institutes to their professors who would then be responsible for their institution's successes and failures; the participation of teachers, students and future employers in the administration of the university; the removal of much decision-making and financial control from Paris to local *recteurs*. Such proposals indicate where the shoe was felt to pinch.

There can be no doubt that at the political level the financial demands of the university competed with the other expensive programmes of the government. But institutional and social obstacles too stood in the way of change. A more 'democratic' university drawing its students in more equitable proportions from the different social classes could only be achieved thanks to the reform of the primary and secondary schools. Already nearly all of those who pass the *baccalauréat* enter the university. The secondary schools are slowly developing orientation procedures. But increasingly it appears that the factors determining a pupil's success in secondary school are to be found in his social environment and in his home; it is in the primary school that adequate compensatory action must be taken. Meantime the university has been unclear about the priority to be accorded to its various tasks; the promotion of the mass, the supply of technical and professional manpower, the development of cultured persons, the selection of an élite, the advancement of research. Its education has been abstract, general and magisterial, delivered in magnificently prepared series of lectures by professors who had the *agrégé's* contempt for and ignorance of pedagogy, and a well-developed taste for his subject rather than for his student.

One attempt, among many—for Frenchmen have long been aware of the deficiencies of their institutions and have exposed them courageously—to see the problems in a large perspective was made in the same enquiry (*Esprit*, 1964) by M. Jacques Berque, who offered an anthropological definition of education, 'Education is the totality of relationships between youth and adult society.' He then continued:

> Straightaway there emerge the vices of our present system: its unilateral character (everything is organized and conceived in relation to the society of adults whose childhood and youth are only looked on as a preparatory annexe); the neglect of those values that belong to youth, which we only imagine, at best, by relating them to or even setting them in opposition to those of adults, whereas they really exist in themselves . . .

But the attempt to turn attention to students' needs and values, and the hope of introducing new perspectives by the appointment of young professors and lecturers in large numbers have been frustrated by a major fact of rigidity: the capacity of an institution to enrol large numbers of students who do not actually have to attend lectures and seminars. Some control over entry seems indicated, but this does not harmonize easily with 'democratization', nor with the social pressure of 'demand', nor with the economy's need for highly educated manpower. What was more strongly urged was diversification. There should, said the reformers, be many more levels of higher education. There should be many more options and combinations of disciplines. There could even be clear distinctions of prestige between universities and university colleges. Different institutions could prepare students for different diplomas and degrees. And examinations should be used not just to record a success or a failure but as a test to be taken into account in guiding a student into the next choice of several ways open to him. It was admitted that an examination also selects for a higher stage of study or research but it was argued that it should not be the only test of capacity for research, nor should any student be faced, subsequent to examination, with blank failure leading nowhere—or even with blank success leading to no employment.

The provision of outlets for students implies, of course, greater links between the universities and the consumers of their products. The university, protected but dependent and not autonomous, protected but isolated and not productive, was said often to be 'camping in the nation', i.e. to be living off the nation (not very opulently), to be surrounded by walls, to be contributing irrelevant products and to be overcrowded. Change implied the sort of planning that takes account of the primacy of research, of the different levels and kinds of achievement to be promoted, of the students' desires. These are: to grow as persons enjoying a rich cultural heritage, to be employable and to be consulted. Such a change would require a change of mentality and an increase of resources. Voices were not wanting to warn Frenchmen of the dangers of pursuing incompatible policies, and of not making a political decision. M. Paul Ricoeur, for example, summing up the remarkable debate in the journal *Esprit*, wrote about the task of making the University:

Making the University—it is now up to the nation to will it. But the nation must know that if it wants a large University with unlimited access—and that seems to be what it wants— then the only institution that will be viable on these terms will be expensive, very expensive. If the University is to guide rather than to eliminate and is at the same time to proceed to continuous selection with a view to research, then it must in the next few years receive considerable grants. But this choice has never been clearly made by the country; it has not even been put to it. But this choice must be set against all the others: the rate of growth, the nuclear strike force, leisure consumption, European politics, aid to the Third World, etc. The dossier of choice—to which this present document is our contribution—must be set forth and discussed publicly; the decisions to be taken for or against these great alternatives must be knowingly incorporated into a grand policy and explained to the country by both opposition and government. If this country does not, by this reasoned choice, regulate the growth of the University then it will experience the education explosion as a national cataclysm.

Steps towards reform

It was a year later, in May 1965, that M. Christian Fouchet presented his series of reformatory measures including some redesigning of higher education. In place of the one introductory year (*année propédeutique*) of study tested by an eliminatory examination, he introduced as the first of three stages of university education a two-year cycle leading to a diploma in literary or scientific studies. In the literary faculties of all universities six main sections were envisaged 'according to the national plan' as being specially relevant to those preparing to teach—classics, modern studies, foreign languages, history, geography and philosophy—and three other special sections for those students interested in psychology, sociology or the history of art and archaeology. A further year of study then led to the *licence* required for secondary school teachers, and two years of study led to a newly introduced *maîtrise* or master's degree. Beyond that level candidates entering the third cycle prepared for a doctorate or for the competitively won distinction of *agrégation*. A similar system of cycles operated in the science faculties, to which, however, initial access was only granted to students whose *baccalauréat* subjects included the requisite mathematics or natural science.

M. Fouchet's other main innovation was the creation of university institutes of technology for the training of highly specialized technicians with more general education than the normal technician, with enough general understanding to be able to co-operate with higher management and engineers, and enough special skill to translate their plans into operations. For the university, this did represent the acceptance of a new function: the training of skilled personnel in civil engineering, mechanical construction, dynamics, electronics and automation, chemistry, laboratory management, applied biology, administration, local government, documentation and statistics. Of the 750,000 post-*baccalauréat* students forecast for 1972 by the Fifth Plan, the authorities reckoned that a quarter would be following these courses. So a new set of qualifications with clearly professional outlets was decreed (actually the decree was dated 7 January 1966) and institutes were established of various kinds in twelve provincial universities as well as in Paris. It all represented a step towards carefully graded levels of achievement, the acceptance of training for intermediate management, the diversification of special institutes and the preparation of students for recognizable employment. A step towards greater financial autonomy for the National Scientific Research Centre was also taken: modifications of its agreed budget need only be approved if these involved an increase in its total, or the switching of funds between 'personnel' and 'material' or between 'operations' and 'equipment'; and a special credit amounting to 7·5 million francs was put at the Centre's disposal for unforeseen or urgent needs, to be used without prior checks by the Ministry's accountants. It was pointed out that this latter step was a great departure from the traditional principle of *prior* control over the allocation of credits, but that the experiment might be extended to other research organs. No mention was yet made in this connection of universities as a whole.

From the Ministry's point of view, these reforms constituted a significant response to various pressures and a recognition of the universities' triple function: research, transmission of knowledge and training up to different levels of expertise. A rather cool reception was extended by other observers. M. Jean Capelle, for example, feared that the university, having renounced the selection of entrants, wanted to separate the grain from the chaff and to draw off the poorer students from the faculties into the institutes, and he doubted whether technically competent people could really be trained in an atmosphere so remote from the realities of industry (1966, p. 211).

Other observers had serious questions to put, while admitting that the development initiated by the Ministry was in the right general direction. The separation of research workers from future teachers after two years of a common course was on the whole welcomed by scientists, but questioned by arts students and graduates. It seemed to be a step towards the establishment of a new hierarchy: research course, future teachers' course, institute of technology. Many teachers regretted too the implied separation of future university work and of secondary school teaching, for in the past the *professeurs* in either a *lycée* or a university faculty enjoyed equal prestige and were interchangeable. It would, however, be difficult for the holder of a *licence* to transform himself into a success-ful candidate for the master's degree in one year. The division be-tween the future élite of research workers and the general output of undistinguished *licenciés* seemed to be premature. And the future preparation of *professeurs* in colleges of general education seemed to have been left out of account altogether. Such observations are important indications of underlying anxiety about their status and training, felt by the students and professional associations outside the science and medical faculties. To these indications of dissatis-faction the federation of parents of pupils in various kinds of schools added its comment, pointing out that the Minister had said nothing about new syllabuses, new pedagogical methods and new financial credits for the training and remuneration of teachers.

Some reefs on which the reform might run aground were foreseen by the Secretary-General of the Ministry. These were: the continua-tion of selection on the basis of failure at the end of the first year of university study (54 per cent of students registered in the faculties of arts, and 56 per cent of those registered in the science faculties, either failed to sit or did not pass the examination in 1963); the growing distortion of the university intake in relation to what society might absorb—less than a third of the students following courses in 1964-5 were in science faculties; and the continuing shortage of engineers and higher technicians. These obstacles to smooth development of the universities certainly existed; but the proposed responses from the Minister can hardly be said to have been com-mensurate in vigour and imagination with the frustration and apprehension that such a state of affairs could be assumed to have aroused in the minds of students.

Defending himself at the Caen colloquium of university teachers which met in November 1966 to consider the reform of higher education, the Minister put his finger on a crucial difference between political action and academic debate. 'You', he said, 'have an advantage over me . . . You are in the absolute and I am in the relative.' He went on to describe his task as 'to fix a policy of development for the university in harmony with the progress of the nation'. Basic to this was 'the art of the possible', and he did not think it was appropriate to sweep away what already existed. In the light of revolutionary activity by students eighteen months later this comment is worth remembering, for it was later contended by some students that no real reform could be achieved unless a good deal of destruction of existing structures first took place. Their disruptive activity may be interpreted as an attempt to change the basic terms in which the puzzles of reform were posed: how much? how quickly? on whose behalf? The Minister himself hoped for rapid evolution rather than revolution. He ruled out any easy solution borrowed from a foreign country, remarking that 'the university of a country is an image of its society.' This too the students were to agree with and to turn into a major complaint rather than a line of defence.

In its final report the colloquium proposed an outline for new university structures. It rejected the idea of one national structure with identical regional establishments as being an arrangement more suited to the post office or the police or the primary school system. Universities in the plural had to be created, and these should be both different from one another and autonomous in matters of policy and administration. The function of the Ministry would be to see that such universities were adequately financed, equipped and staffed. The universities would determine their own modes of admission, teaching, examination or assessment and guidance towards a variety of courses and outlets. Any examination would test work done and would not be prognostic but should be linked with some entry door into society. The professors should be grouped in departments, schools, institutes and laboratories, and should elect their university president for a period of three years.

Further debate

Fifteen months later and just two months before the violent up-heaval of the University in May and June 1968, the current of words and ideas was flowing even more strongly at the Amiens Colloquium when 500 participants invited by the *Association d'étude pour l'expansion de la recherche scientifique* met to pool the findings of their study groups with regard particularly to secondary education. The different levels at which participants considered the subject indicate its complexity.

The Minister of National Education, who was M. Alain Peyrefitte (he resigned after the riots a few months later), spoke truisms about the rapid mutation of French society, the failure of educational institutions to keep pace and the fact that education no longer had any 'bite'. Young people had to learn to live with change, anxiety, uncertainty and to develop a sense of criticism, irony, autonomy and sociability. Relationships between masters and pupils were in need of renovation, and so were the training of teachers and the methods of the classroom.

Attempting to clarify the objectives of education M. Gilles Ferry started from the contradiction between traditional aims that persisted and new aims that were badly integrated into the system, with the result that the role of the teacher was unclear. The traditional conception of culture held it to be intellectual and encyclopaedic; humanism was disengaged and free from vocational taint; the school was open to all and its hierarchy was then determined by 'merit' which was presumed to be unaffected by socio-economic inequalities; liberty was held to be neutral, and it was up to the child to make sense of his discrete parcels of knowledge just as it was up to the family to inculcate values that would give the pupil a basis on which to form attitudes. The new tasks of the school include, said M. Ferry, preparation for wage-earning and the recognition in secondary courses of a variety of forms of intelligence; the pupil is no longer to be seen as an intellect only but also as a body with potential skills and expressions; he will have to be adaptable and he will want to participate anxiously in his own process of education. Contradictory interpretations confuse the act of teaching and the image and rule of the teacher. He teaches alone in front of his class but is expected to act as one of a team. He is intelligent and articulate but takes no part in the running of the school. He is well-informed but seems uninterestingly remote from the world revealed by television and successful wage-earning. He is expected to innovate, but his attempts to introduce '*classes nouvelles*' or 'observation' are rejected by the system. M. Ferry then referred to the country's inability to override these contradictions. It may be that the student riots of the early summer were an attempt to alter one set of terms by eliminating much of the traditional structure (*Education Nationale*, 19 April 1968).

The commission on the evolution of the structure of establishments reported to the Amiens colloquium that the present structures were ill-suited for the new tasks. Moral and artistic education were missing. The information imparted was too bookish. The teaching emphasized content rather than methods. Competition reigned in the classroom. Essays led to classification as a good pupil or a dunce. Examination brooded heavily over the class, and determined the system of elimination. The teacher had little contact with the world outside his books and his pupils, and tended to see his service in terms of the regulation fifteen or eighteen hours a week plus research and correction: while the pupil was burdened with a weekly load occupying between twenty-five and forty-four hours. The new structures should place the secondary school in the context of further and adult education, should reduce the emphasis on individual brilliance and permit greater individual variety of pace and aptitude, and should organize the basic content of the syllabus over longer, less constricting, cyclical periods rather than in annual slices. Teachers should work in teams, and demolish the partitions between subject disciplines. Along with teachers there should act as participants in the educational enterprise the representatives of parents, pupils and cultural organizations. Secondary schools would become district schools, each type succeeding rather than competing with each other. Each school unit should limit its intake to 600 pupils, and be largely responsible for its own financial and academic policies. Any official control should operate after a school had taken action, not before. The functions of the head of the school would be to foresee, co-ordinate, stimulate, conduct external relations, implement the policy of the establishment as agreed between himself and colleagues. And as the school should also act as a cultural centre for the locality, its architecture should be redesigned.

The class as a unit was criticized too for its inflexibility, and even 'orientation' was admitted to be a too rigid system whereby pupils were switched along one of several tracks without the possibility of delayed decision or of a change of direction.

It was clearly seen that such developments implied pedagogical training for all teachers, preferably in a university course. But immediately a problem of structure became apparent to the colloquium: the first cycle of secondary pupils requires many-sided teachers capable of taking various subjects, but the university is not geared to training such graduates. Should the structure of the university faculties be changed to accommodate something approaching the American 'credits' system? Oddly enough, it was the scientists who, having called the colloquium, saw difficulties in such a reform since they are content with the present system of options presented to science students and with the opportunity the system gives for building up cumulative scientific knowledge. So there is opposition among the university teachers to any diversification of the first cycle in the secondary schools—an extremely interesting demonstration of the unity of the whole educational system and of the uncomfortable pressure which one section is bound to exert upon another as they try to realign themselves within the same framework. But the framework was too constricting to allow of much adjustment, and certainly it precluded the entry of a new force for whom the nation had not planned: the students themselves. The irruption of a new force to be reckoned with necessarily cracked the structure and threatened at times to demolish it.

Revolt by the students

Student demonstrations were taking place in many parts of the world in the spring of 1968 as a new and numerous generation, increasingly conscious both of their future value to society and of their present exclusion from effective participation in decisions affecting their nation's policies in the world and in their universities, discovered techniques for opposing authority, for disrupting normal order and for winning public sympathy. Some of these demonstrations were related to the readjustment of political power in the world, and the opening of peace talks in Paris between representatives of North Vietnam and of the United States added topicality to the activities of those small groups of students and *lycées* whose sympathies were violently revolutionary. Some of the demonstrations had limited purposes related only to the educational structures of France. These enlisted the active support of teachers and professors too, as in the case of the strike called in May by the associations of teachers in technical schools to underline their demands for a greater share of the 1969 educational budget so that more staff and equipment could be provided. In Paris the National Union of French Students (UNEF) with the support of the General Confederation of Labour (CGT) and of the Communist Party and the Councils of Parents of Pupils, organized at the end of March a demonstration and strike as part of a campaign for more serious planning and more rapid construction of new premises.

Planning in France does not control the intake of students and production of graduates, though forecasts attempt to relate them to the demands of the national economy. Nor is planning adequately translated from its conceptual stage to its material implementation. The planners may prescribe a certain output of scientists, but the great influx of students is still into the faculties of letters and human sciences and of law and economic sciences. Emergency action taken in 1964 did give rise to the new faculties in Nanterre on the outskirts of Paris. The new buildings were quickly overfull, accommodating some 14,000 students by 1968. Elsewhere in the Paris region the main buildings being constructed were for science students and some of these partially completed buildings were already accommodating more students than they were supposed to receive when finally ready. The dean of the faculty of science in Paris reported (Gaussen, 1968) that he had been asked urgently for his development plans in 1962, and that six years later the Ministry had still not completed the acquisition of the land on which to build. Meantime the restiveness of students in Nanterre and the uncertainty about how to develop reforms already introduced—whether to build more university technical institutes or more university faculties, and if the latter then whether to take into account recommendations from the Caen colloquium about interdisciplinary faculties— contributed to a further lack of dynamic planning.

A generally explosive mixture of grievances existed, and it was in Nanterre that the fuse was lit which led to detonation in the centre of Paris. Students in Nanterre were already angry about restrictions on visiting between men and women, and on the use of university premises for political activity. They complained that the Fouchet reforms had been too precipitately applied, that the new syllabuses were excessively burdensome, especially for students of letters, that their complaints were not being listened to, that they were being trained in psychology and sociology for posts that did not exist in adequate numbers, and that in any case they did not as psychologists and sociologists want to manipulate their fellows in a society geared for the production and consumption of goods. Teaching facilities were overstrained, and one professor, M. Gilles Ferry, reported that in three years his student classes had risen from eighty to four hundred, making personal acquaintance and supervision impossible. Small groups of left-wing students had broken up classes, interrupted professors, demanded open discussion in place of formal lectures and were extending their campaign to the discussions of a general attack upon bourgeois society and to an appeal to workers generally for sympathy and support of student efforts to overthrow the institutions of society. Scuffles had taken place in the faculty buildings, and in the city itself students had been arrested on 22 March (a date which subsequently gave its name to the violent student movement emanating from Nanterre) who were demonstrating outside the American Express building against the American military action in Vietnam. At the end of March a students' debate on freedom of expression was planned to take place in the Nanterre buildings which the dean then declared closed for two days, and early in May some 'anti-imperialist demonstrations' ended in such disorder that the faculty was closed altogether. The excluded students then betook themselves to the Sorbonne. The *recteur* of Paris and the dean of the Sorbonne called in the police to evacuate the university buildings and to clear the near-by streets. This act, likened by M. Raymond Aron to the waving of a red rag before a bull, led to a vast movement of anger and sympathy in which students and teachers protested against the intrusion of police into the university, and then to a series of massive marches and demonstrations culminating in the erection of barricades and in violent fights between students and the police riot squads. The Prime Minister M. Pompidou was abroad and the President, General de Gaulle, was about to pay a state visit to Roumania. By the time the latter returned, the street battles and demonstrations were backed by massive national strikes for higher wages, greater participation in factory control and a change of government. The movement was approaching revolutionary proportions in Paris, and even the President's offer of a referendum was received with derision. He withdrew it, offered new general elections instead, and as strikers took what gains they could get and returned to work the conservative forces reformed in Paris and in the provinces to win the elections in June by a massive majority.

But for two months the educational institutions of the country did in fact live through a potentially revolutionary period in which the various pressures at work displayed themselves most revealingly. The student revolutionary groups, at first getting a very cool reception from striking workers and a very cautious one from the Communist Party leaders who suspected an initiative they did not control and a revolutionary situation they had not fully prepared, had no clear long-term political programme. But there may well have been insight in the remark of one of their leaders, M. Daniel Cohn-Bendit, who, taxed with this lack of clarity, said, '*Bougeons d'abord. La théorie du mouvement viendra après*' (Let's move first. The theory of movement will come later). His was in fact an attempt to change the terms in which the problem of reform was set. He rejected the adjustments that were possible within the existing framework of institutions and aimed to create movement that would wreck at least some of them. Rebuilding without prior destruction no longer seemed possible to some of the students. Another important expression of opinion was the view that one's aims and programmes were less important than the means one employed and the company one kept. Out of flux, dialogue, endless discussion, slogans, student newspapers, seminars and working parties set up by students and professors, and even in many *lycées* by the older pupils and their teachers, there would—it was hoped—gradually emerge both the projects and the means. Talk, discussion, participation and joint working parties controlling the use of premises and the publication of findings became ends as well as means, compensating perhaps for the decades of passivity endured by students hearkening to the well-delivered magisterial course of lessons or lectures. The talk ranged beyond problems of university organization, for students and teachers were agreed that the university's function was to make an impact on society rather than to adapt to it uncritically.

Professors and teachers met also to pass resolutions and turn to account the power of the students' movement and the vacillation of the government during the month of May. The science professors of Paris called for university autonomy, the recasting of the outmoded Napoleonic framework that links the university through its *recteur* and the local prefect to the central administration, and the election of each university's head by the members of the university. The deans of the faculties of letters met in Lille to condemn the inadequacy of plans and of their implementation, and to denounce the 'mania for centralization' which could only conceive of one university structure for Paris and the provinces. They proclaimed the need for a variety of institutions dedicated to research, invested with powers of initiative and self-government, and prepared to revise both the content and the teaching methods of their programmes. The deans also offered their collective resignation if sufficient reassurances about the size of the financial credits to be granted were not forthcoming within a month. The University of Strasbourg proclaimed its 'autonomy' and was followed by other provincial faculties. So a whole movement of decentralization and a prospect of regional federalism contrary to both the monarchical and republican traditions of France were given institutional expression, if only temporarily. Not all the talk about 'autonomy' was ill-advised or utopian. Rectors and professors recognized that they would have to operate within a budget granted by the State and that sufficient co-ordination must exist to ensure that the degree of one French university continued to be equivalent to that of another. What was sought was freedom and rapidity of action within the general budgetary limits, a certain competitiveness between universities and the freedom of students to seek enrolment in the university of their choice.

The size of various university units would have to be such as would permit continuing human contact. Each university unit would be allowed to work out for itself its own relationships to its technical institutes and junior colleges (if it wished to establish them), and to determine what boundaries if any were to remain between subject faculties or departments within the university. In particular it was argued that the executive control exercised by the university teachers and students in such enterprises as student welfare services should be extended so that the heads of schools and faculties could decide what kind of new buildings would be erected.

The collusion of the Ministries of National Education and of Finance to prevent the building of halls, clubs, cinemas, etc., for use by the students was especially deplored. The terms of such joint control as would allow teachers and students to take part in decisions would, it was recognized, have to be worked out in conversations between them and the civil servants.

The problem of selection also received attention. The Minister had just appointed a commission to examine this problem, and as its chairman had nominated M. Jean Capelle who was known to favour some degree of selection. In his view the *baccalauréat* examination should test the work of the secondary school, and further tests relevant to the special subjects a prospective student proposed to study should be sat by every candidate for entry to a higher institution. Serious efforts to guide future students would therefore have to be built into the work of the secondary schools, and the numbers admitted to each course would have to bear some relation to the number of outlets into industry. The alternative view, held by most students and hotly advocated by them during these months of demonstration, contested the need for selection and advocated serious efforts at orientation during the years of university study, so as to minimize the risks of unemployment, but they also deprecated any suggestion of narrow vocational preparation designed to fit them into suspiciously ready openings in the adult world of commerce and industry.

Those educationalists who had criticized the examination systems also took the opportunity to restate their case. Opposition to examinations took several forms. Some would have eliminated all forms of set examination. Some declared the *baccalauréat* to have lost its value. Some questioned the relevance of the *agrégation*, complaining that as a teaching qualification it guaranteed only the ability to deliver a well-constructed lecture and was therefore irrelevant in the new pedagogical situation in schools, and that as a higher university qualification it did not guarantee the ability to initiate research and was therefore irrelevant to the needs of the universities. Some deplored the amount of time examinations demanded of students and teachers and the consequent curtailment of hours available for teaching. Some contended that examinations confirmed who were the best and the poorest candidates but were an uncertain measure of the great numbers between the extremes. For days the twin problems of examination and selection occupied the attention of students and teachers in the groups and committees that met in rooms, amphitheatres and courtyards. This concentration upon the examination system was not fortuitous. Those students who were restive because no career lay clearly open to them resented a system which could eliminate them or which might accord them the university's approval without guaranteeing its value in monetary terms. Those students who were rebelling against a society they were being trained to understand and manipulate rather than to reject and reconstruct were, in refusing the examinations, declining the established *rites de passage*. The two groups of students felt themselves to be peripheral. The second group was smaller and might not have carried the anxious career-minded majority along with it had the authorities in Nanterre or in the Sorbonne felt able to face further days of interruption and disturbance until the majority of students felt themselves clearly threatened. The closure of the faculty, the legal action threatened against student agitators, the invitation to the police to protect the Sorbonne sparked off a reaction of anger which unified, for the month of May, various groups of students and some teachers in demonstrations of protest. But even at the height of student wrath, while young *lycéens* joined the strike and refused to sit the *baccalauréat*, their parents' councils expressed the hope that examinations could take place normally. They also took advantage of the occasion to restate their claims: that senior pupils should be allowed some responsibilities in the running of schools, and that the experience of *lycées-pilotes* should be generalized. Other groups acted similarly.

The *société des agrégés* proclaimed the need for more teachers with that qualification, for more subsidized places in the universities' institutes registering students who intend to teach, for passes to be granted to more candidates in the competitive examinations for a teaching qualification and for insistence on public competitive examinations as the channel for filling newly created teaching posts in secondary schools or university faculties. The organization for the *Défense de la jeunesse scolaire* emphasized the new possibilities now opened for the introduction of various 'progressive' practices, the reduction of the size of classes, and the extension of the primary teacher's professional pedagogical training from one to two years.

Gradually the more conservative interpretation of student unrest prevailed: that the university structure was outmoded and that the solution lay in adaptation rather than in the radical transformation of a prosperous consumers' society. Sober minds drew attention to two recurring aspects of an educational process punctuated by examinations. First, there was no way of caring for those who failed an examination; reorientation was inadequately organized. Second, the difficulties were really most acute for the students of letters, or sociology, or psychology; these subjects had an attractive cultural and generally educational value, but offered correspondingly poor guarantee of employment. An interim aim could be the establishment of equilibrium between the numbers admitted and the resources available in rooms, libraries, laboratories and teaching staff: this would pose a large enough task for a year or two. But ultimately arrangements must be made for the distribution of secondary school leavers into work or training or further education by the provision of a large range of options to compensate for the severity of selection at that point; or else similar alternative routes must be offered as students freely admitted dropping out of university courses, eliminated by academic demands and periodic examinations. Advice and guidance must, it was agreed in many discussions, be given sympathetically or knowledgeably by persons, not through impersonal instructions; and this in turn would mean the training and employment of counsellors not yet supplied in any significant numbers. Gradually, as the debate proceeded, issues became clarified if not solved, and gradually too the anxious voices of parents and of some students whose professional qualifications were being delayed by the disruption of examinations were increasingly heard. Postponement rather than abolition of examinations was agreed upon. Somehow, perhaps because the students lacked both a political programme and political power, and because the Communist Party took no unconstitutional action so that in the critical last ten days of May no alternative government stepped in to topple a régime that seemed to have lost all confidence, the obstinacy of the President, his warning about the danger of totalitarianism and the growing fears of law-abiding citizens enabled the machinery of order to start moving again. Barricades were dismantled and the Sorbonne and the Odéon theatre emptied of students. Political and educational conservativism reasserted itself as twin aspects of the Fifth Republic, at least during the respite offered by the summer vacation. The workers returned from strike, pleased with their economic gains and the promise of greater 'participation', and the Gaullist supporters won an overall majority in the June elections. The schoolteachers returned to duty having won from the Minister promises of a budget that would pay for 16,000 more teaching posts than had been planned for the year 1968-9, of firm limits to the size of classes and of working parties to study problems of teacher training and of union affiliation. The *lycéens* who had worked out radical propositions along with their striking teachers declared that of course they would sit their *baccalauréat* examinations, that they had never really meant to boycott them, that their objections had only been 'in principle' and that they had had to make exorbitant demands in order to win small concessions. Candidates sat the examinations at the end of June, were leniently assessed and presented themselves for university courses in embarrassingly large numbers in the autumn.

Yet the revolt against the Plan had been in fact at much more fundamental levels. The whole function of society had been questioned, and the role of the university in it. A serious effort had been made to link dissenting students with dissatisfied workers and for a time their joint revolt had taken the government by surprise and threatened it. This union of protesting young bourgeois and demanding young workers did not last, partly because the latter had to return to wage-earning, partly because their demands were easier to satisfy by a prompt increase of salaries plus a promise of greater participation; and partly because the students were concerned with the criticism of the culture they were being invited to enter, with the abolition of capitalist society, with the needs of the 'third world', with joint student–teacher control in autonomous universities that did not yet exist and with measures for the democratization of the university that would permit a fair proportion of workers' children to enter it. These were long-term aims. Nevertheless, it had been demonstrated that not only industrial workers could initiate an urgent mass movement. The demographic and education explosions in France had produced a body of educands large enough to constitute a 'mass' and conscious enough of their numbers to use them strategically. It had been shown too that the university in general must continue to harbour a group of students and professors whom structural adaptations and more generous budgets would not satisfy, and who would continue to call into question the traditional neutrality of the university in ideological matters.

By mid-June the occupied university buildings had been cleared of students, the government had banned several Trotskyist and Maoist groups whose aims included either disruption of order or forcible seizure of control. Various university *recteurs* had warned students that further damage to property or persons would be treated as matters for the police. In *lycées* and in university faculties 'autonomous' groups of teachers, not affiliated to any politically active union, had formed to protest against the intrusion of political struggles for power into educational issues and to direct attention to the more limited problems of pedagogical content and method. Many university teachers, responding to the plea of M. Raymond Aron in *Le Figaro*, combined to condemn demagogic pressure such as the interruption of classes, the intimidation of professors and the passing of resolutions by a public show of hands in assemblies that were not truly representative. He argued strongly in favour of reform by discussion in groups that had been carefully elected, that would respect the university's belief in rational debate and that would vote in secret ballot on contentious issues.

7

Response from the Government

Such a careful but concerned interpretation of the university's immediate need for a return to rationality cannot be equated with President de Gaulle's understanding of the position when, in a speech made early in June 1968, he taxed the university with having failed to reform itself. The relationship of a university to a government may not be that of a competitor for power, but when various *professeurs* protested eventually against the political aims that students had introduced into what was initially a university dilemma, they were not so naïve as to suppose that there was no political side to university reform. The university as a public body could obviously only be reformed with governmental co-operation. And the President's assurance that the university would in future be so organized as to ensure a professional outlet for all graduates responded only to the anxiety of part of the student body and failed to recognize this other equally deep concern lest the university should lose its critical role and its service in broadening the minds of students as well as equipping them vocationally. The new Minister's interpretation of the revolt could be deduced from his proposals made a week later, of which a summary follows.

It was important, said M. Faure, to listen to students and to try to understand their discontent. The Napoleonic concept of the single centralized hierarchical university was outmoded. Democratization was essential, from the nursery schools right through to the universities. This implied new methods of teaching and of examination that would not favour some social groups and handicap others. The passes in the June session of the *baccalauréat* had risen from 49·9 per cent in 1967 to 65·8 per cent in 1968, and this meant that 80,000 new students would have to be accommodated in that October, of these 10,000 to 15,000 being in the Paris region. The government would see that this was done. New university units must be established in time, and must have 'personality'; each would not exceed 10,000 or 12,000 students. New posts would be created for the various servicing departments of universities: libraries, laboratories, copying services, etc. No selection procedure would be introduced since there did not yet exist channels into which the rejected candidates could be diverted; emphasis would be laid rather on good qualification and on orientation in relation to it. Attention would be given to the relationships between the teachers and the taught, and between teachers and bureaucrats. An enabling law would be tabled in September outlining relationships between the State and various institutions, the limits of autonomy and suitable forms of representation. Such venerable university traditions as the immovable professor, and the doctoral thesis occupying up to ten years of preparation should be queried. Regional university councils of students and teachers might also find room for the representatives of industry: this was a delicate matter. The growth of autonomy would be gradual. Certainly control over a budget should be related to objectives clearly defined in advance rather than to the later detailed checking of accounts. But autonomous universities should not enter into competition with one another, nor should any hierarchy of universities or their degrees be allowed to develop. Students should determine the modes of their own social life in university hostels and halls.

With regard to secondary education, M. Faure said that examinations should assist the acquisition of knowledge; most candidates should pass them; none should spend years preparing desperately to pass a competitive examination. There was still need to break down partitions in secondary education, so the first cycle of two years should in fact be used for observation and orientation, the introduction of Latin being postponed until the third year. Even then, the curriculum should continue to offer a '*tronc commun*' of basic subjects, with options such as Latin, technology, more history or geography. A balanced curriculum of studies in science and in letters should be pursued throughout the school, allowing the university candidate to choose his own course fairly freely. The upper secondary classes, being already 'students', should be taught elements of law, political economy and political ideas, and be introduced to problems of marriage, divorce, accounts, making one's will; and should acquire some practical familiarity with engines. Too much reliance had been put upon memory as opposed to understanding or reflexion. The examination system had been too arbitrary; since not all knowledge could be tested, the setting of questions had increasingly depended on chance or on a teacher's hobby-horse. Less should depend on the fortunes of examination day, and more autonomy be given to schools in the matter of assessment. Their purpose was not to confirm the existence of an élite, but to improve those pupils whose gifts were not exceptional. A second vice was the '*cours magistral*', the lecture delivered by some and passively received by others. Teaching should include more elements of research and discussion. A third fault of the system was that its eyes were closed to the world. The students who revolted in May and June had at least tried to make contact with the workers. Greater participation would overcome the sense of alienation, and the consumer society so derided by the students as inadequate could develop into the *société de promotion*.

M. Faure had, of course, not satisfied the left wing of the National Assembly; but his sympathetic approach to the insurgent students made the right wing of his own party (UDR) very uneasy. The communist Deputy who spoke after M. Faure called for the election of the principal of each university to replace the *recteur*, for co-ordination of universities within a national plan lest private universities should develop as private schools had done, for a single corps of teachers, for continuous assessment of full-time students in place of many examinations and for large supplementary credits. It was observed too, by other speakers and commentators, that M. Faure had made no explicit reference to the reforms of 1966 introduced by M. Fouchet, but that his silence on these changes, which many *lycéens* had found restricting and many students had found precipitate, was eloquent. Presumably the *baccalauréat* courses which M. Fouchet had limited in number in an attempt to streamline the work of the final two years at school would now give way to a variety of options in a generally balanced curriculum.

Outside the National Assembly, the resuscitation of the term *tronc commun* and the reference to the removal of some partitions in secondary schools were interpreted as an important concession to the *Comité National d'Action laïque* and an attempt to promote further democratization. But M. Faure had been silent on the question of church schools, and this silence was regretted by zealously secular students and teachers. Even the more moderate students interpreted the speech as 'reform from above' and threatened direct participation in the autumn if students were not brought into discussions about employment, training of teachers and competitive universities. The militant *Syndicat National de l'Enseignement Supérieur*, modifying its disapproval of government sufficiently to ask for a discussion with the Minister, was—to the dismay of M. Faure's conservative colleagues and of the moderate 'autonomous' groups of university teachers—received by him. According to its communiqué, the *SNESup* received from the Minister his reassurance that it was normal for students and teachers to engage in politics on university premises. The Minister denied that the government was acting two-facedly, repressing insurgents on the one hand and inviting co-operation on the other. He apparently agreed with his colleague the Minister of the Interior that the repression of disorder was a government matter, and also invited the *SNESup* to take part in various working parties. The *SNESup* reversed the order of events, and summoned the government to demonstrate a policy of pacification and amnesty, thus creating the essential political climate for any useful discussion.

There can be no doubt that the issue of university reform had set problems that were now openly recognized as political; that the university teachers were divided between the new radical aggressive militancy and the old radical defensive neutrality; that the majority party in the National Assembly was already experiencing that tension and division of the centre which controversy over education had produced in previous Republics; and that a requirement of effective planning must be the financial credits to pay for libraries, reading-rooms and staff as well as for physical accommodation.

The law and its interpretation

The law as finally adopted by the National Assembly and the Senate, and promulgated by the President in November 1968 was entitled *la loi d'orientation de l'enseignement supérieur* (law on the orientation of higher education). The word 'orientation' may have a dual significance for the law both laid down the guidelines for future developments to be made known in decrees and circulars, and it stressed that the university process was to be one of guidance rather than of pre-selection or of harsh elimination. 'The University' in its older global sense was now replaced by 'the universities' operating as multi-disciplinary institutions with their own councils on which are represented local interests, teachers and students. Some financial autonomy is assured by the granting of a general budget to each university within which it has some freedom of manoeuvre, and by the elimination of prior ministerial consent before budgeted expenditure is incurred. Each university is expected to develop its own international links, and may appoint foreign professors and lecturers to its staff. It may also develop its own bias or speciality, so long as it contains several disciplines and tries to combine 'as far as possible' (this law is very cautious and not at all specific on many matters) the arts, the sciences and the technologies. One plan for the region of Brittany envisaged four universities (three in Rennes and one in Brest) with over 8,000 students each and with associated university institutes of technology for the 'orientation' of those who flounder in more academic courses. One university might specialize in the training of management, another in the preparation of teachers, a third in the biological sciences (including medicine and pharmacy).

The strategy of regional development and of national planning is in the hands of regional councils which evaluate the plans and budgetary requirements and requests put forward by the various universities, and of the national council which is to be consulted and can make suggestions of its own but remains clearly part of the ministerial structure since the Minister is its President and the Ministry provides its supporting services.

Articles dealing with the administration of each university specify the nature of various councils controlling its internal affairs. Students will participate in administration. (At least there is provision for them to do so; but some change of mood from '*contestation*' to '*participation*' will have to take place.) Professors are no longer to wield their former powers over the use of rooms, laboratories and personnel; the chairmen of various units and departments will be elected for a limited period of office.

Studies leading to national diplomas and degrees will be regulated by the Minister and the National Council. The teaching body of the universities will assess the students 'regularly and continuously'; and examinations will offer a supplementary guide to aptitude. In addition, universities may offer their own special diplomas and administer the courses leading to these local qualifications.

Students are to have free access to information about political, social and economic problems, and are to have their own or other designated accommodation for political activity. Propaganda and public disorder are forbidden, as is the misuse of teaching rooms. The two kinds of accommodation are to be distinct 'as far as possible'.

There is no doubt that the implementation of these measures will continue to tax the Minister's diplomacy. The process will be interesting to watch as the various forces of nationalization, rationalization (what about the agricultural schools controlled by another Ministry? and the *Grandes Ecoles*?), contestation, decentralization, regionalization and so on enter into play and are reflected in the continuing flow of decrees and debates that express the progress of reform. The Minister is not free to act as liberally in 1971 as was planned in 1968. His own political right-wing demands order. So do most voters and a majority of students, provided that their emotional sympathies for youthful effervescence and a certain degree of controlled revolution are not offended by a too evident or too large body of police to control it. Some professors hope to return to their normal lecture courses, supported by students who are preparing for examinations and a clearly visible professional career and who would rather the professor took the initiative and prepared the course rather than that they should themselves engage in dialogue and research. Some professors and heads of *lycées* enjoy the process of dialogue and a position of respected leadership. Some are seriously reformist, deplore the constant interruption of work but hesitate to take any steps that could be interpreted as repressive; and they are optimistic or depressed according to temperament and the discomfort of being squeezed between offended colleagues calling for punishment and impatient students calling for more sympathetic teachers. It is probably the best of the teaching profession in both university faculties and in *lycées* who are being exhausted by their willingness to attend innumerable committees and by their conscientious attempt to teach also.

As the old structures, such as faculties and professorial fiefs, are dismantled or redesigned to make way for new 'teaching units' presided over by elected chairmen who must be acceptable to both radical and conservative electors and who may not therefore be very forceful, it is not clear whether the disintegration is a necessary prelude to new creative mutations or is a lamentable balkanization of the *Université*. It is certain, however, that activity in the faculties or the *lycées* will be watched by the *recteur* who will often react less as a pedagogue than as a political figure, calling in police, or closing a *lycée*; for the issues divide groups in society as they divide the minds of many individual Frenchmen. And behind the reactions of both students and teachers, even to these reforms which they clamoured or worked for over many years, lies the university's general hostility to Gaullist power and consequently to those gifts—be they in the form of the middle school, or of new constitutions for *lycées*, or of new powers for more autonomous universities—which the teacher–student body feels it should properly have accepted only from the hands of a more visibly democratic government. It may turn out too that, since the massive conservative vote recorded in June 1968 encouraged the moderate students in the *Grandes Ecoles* and in the more clearly vocational *Facultés*, and as it strengthened the professors and deans who earlier challenged the validity of the proposals put forward by the Caen colloquium and who opposed the agitation of the *SNESup*, then the structures of the *Facultés* and of professorial controls will be less easily dismantled than the law appears to assume. A new gap between the verbal norm and the institutional implementation may appear.

The pre-1969 *université* in a provincial town was a group of *Facultés*. It had no budget of its own, and really only met as the *université* when the deans of the *Facultés* consulted together—which was usually only on disciplinary matters. The new law orienting the universities aimed at a more flexible organization allowing greater freedom to teachers, research workers, students and administrative personnel. So the hundred or so *Facultés* in the twenty-three *académies* were divided provisionally in 1969 into more than 500 possible new units of teaching and research, and these were listed in the *Bulletin Officiel* (9 January 1969). A unit might be a 'department' or an 'institute' or a 'group of laboratories' or a 'research team', each immediately administered by its own elected council. The intention was that as a result of discussion among the representatives of students and of the various grades of teacher, the units would reconstitute themselves into forty new universities. Each university would combine several academic disciplines and might also reflect a bias towards medicine or science or some other field of study. This mode of operation by discussion was in line with the desire of radically minded students and teachers to build new institutions 'from the bottom up'. Whether such a procedure will succeed in giving the new universities significant autonomy and satisfying power will not be clear for some years to come.

By the end of 1970 there were already signs of second thoughts and even of some reaction. Student participation in the elections to choose delegates for the assemblies that drew up each unit's constitution varied from 77 per cent of registered students in the institutes of technology to 42 per cent in the Faculties of arts. The overall average was 52 per cent. The assemblies met in the Spring of 1969 to draft their constitutions within the provisions of the law which were presumed to be wide. These allowed the unit's council to formulate statutes and internal regulations, to organize the unit, to define relationships with other units and to decide how students were to be taught and evaluated. A lengthy period of transition—up to two years—was foreseen in which the old and the new structures might co-exist pending the planning of new administrative arrangements, the erection of new buildings and the gradual passage from dependency upon examinations to the introduction of other forms of assessment and of work credits (*unités de valeur*).

Some proposals from the new teaching and research units were returned to them by the staff of the *recteurs* as being inconsistent with the law; so it became clear with whom the final interpretation lay. Some groups of students and teachers just got on with their own work, ignoring the provisional councils of Faculties, and thus in effect set up new structural divisions. Some students and teachers tired of the recurrent elections for councils and committees at various levels and became disillusioned with an interpretation of 'participation' that seemed to offer only restricted forms of autonomy. Some councils were dismayed to find that their legal responsibility for university premises and for students' conduct therein had removed embarrassing decisions from the Minister and had turned the councils into guardians of law and order. Some units had not defined their constitution satisfactorily enough to be able to open in October for the academic 1970–1; meantime ministerial approval and budgets were held up.

The dilemmas are understandable. An interdisciplinary university may try to bridge the gap between one form of knowledge and another and to re-establish in higher education the ideal of *culture générale*. But some flexibility of courses and some room for movement by students were achieved and more might have been won even within the large traditional Faculties. Pressure from the Minister upon some Faculties of medicine and of science began to be resented in 1970. It was felt that his influence might more usefully have been applied to ensure that no 'university' consisted only of 'letters' or of 'law and letters'. On the other hand, it is understandable that some Faculties should hesitate to yoke themselves with the turbulent students of human sciences, should declare themselves to be a teaching and research unit and should try to win departmental autonomy in budgetary and administrative matters so as to weaken the overall power of the new university. It was already clear from the published list that many institutes and research establishments would retain separate status and that the *Grandes Ecoles* would for some time remain independent even if attached by consent to a university.

One obvious choice open to elected representatives was between units consisting of cycles of study organized by years, and units consisting of Faculties or academic disciplines. Most universities seem to have opted for the latter, thus perpetuating some professorial control and protecting themselves prudently against the absorption of their post-graduate and research work into some other unit organized on a basis of cycles of study. For the students who favoured a broad spectrum of studies in their first year followed by a very gradual and tentative orientation in a second cycle of studies, this organization by separate disciplines may prove to be too rigid and may give rise to further dissatisfaction. The future growth of the new universities must reflect the balance of these pressures for change and for restraint. Meantime it would be legitimate to infer that the conservative nature of the National Assembly at the beginning of the decade of the seventies had encouraged the more traditionally minded of the professors and of the students to interpret the new law less adventurously than its ambiguity permitted. Writing in *Le Monde* (9 September 1970) M. Robert Devril, *Recteur* of the Academy of Nice, said:

The French University was enclosed in too rigid structures—
the Faculties . . . We had a chance to change. But the fears of

certain professors that they might lose prestige or power or might control smaller budgets has meant that even here where we have a new university entity we have not succeeded in making anything new. What we have to change is the outlook of university teachers.

The following lists, valid for the academic year 1970–1, show what groupings resulted from the reorganization.

TABLE 3. The new French universities

Aix-Marseille I	Letters, science, observatory	*Grenoble I*	Medicine, pharmacy, law, science, letters, technology
Aix-Marseille II	Medicine, law, pharmacy, technology, business administration	*Grenoble II*	Law, technology
		Grenoble III	Letters
Amiens	Medicine, pharmacy, science, letters, law, technology	*Lille I*	Business administration, science, technology, data processing
Angers	Medicine, pharmacy, science, letters, technology, law	*Lille II*	Medicine, pharmacy, dentistry, law
		Lille III	Letters
Besançon	Letters, medicine, pharmacy, science, technology, observatory	*Limoges*	Medicine, pharmacy, law, letters, technology
Bordeaux I	Science, law, institute of political sciences	*Lyon I*	Science, observatory, technology, medicine, pharmacy
Bordeaux II	Medicine, pharmacy, letters, science	*Lyon II*	Letters, law, business administration
Bordeaux III	Letters, science, sociology, information	*Le Mans*	Science, letters, law, technology
		Metz	Letters, science, technology
Brest	Medicine, science, letters, technology	*Montpellier I*	Law, business administration, medicine, pharmacy, dentistry
Caen	Medicine, pharmacy, law, science, technology, data processing	*Montpellier II*	Science, technology, business administration
		Montpellier III	Letters
Chambéry	Science, letters	*Mulhouse*	Science, letters, technology
Dijon	Medicine, pharmacy, law, science, technology, observatory	*Nancy I*	Medicine, pharmacy, dentistry, science, technology

TABLE 3 (*continued*)

Nancy II	Law, letters	Rouen	Medicine, pharmacy, law, letters, technology
Nantes	Medicine, pharmacy, dentistry, law, letters, technology	Sainte-Etienne	Science, law, letters, technology, medicine, pharmacy, dentistry
Nice	Medicine, law, letters, technology, business administration	Strasbourg I	Science
		Strasbourg II	Letters
Orléans	Law, data processing, technology	Strasbourg III	Law, journalism, technology
Pau	Law, letters, science	Toulouse I	Law, business administration, data processing
Perpignan	Science		
Poitiers	Medicine, pharmacy, law, technology	Toulouse II	Letters, management
Reims	Medicine, pharmacy, law, letters, technology	Toulouse III	Science, technology, medicine, pharmacy, dentistry
Rennes I	Law, medicine, pharmacy, dentistry, science, technology	Tours	Medicine, pharmacy, letters, law, technology
Rennes II	Letters	Valenciennes	Science, technology

The student revolt and the industrial strikes of May and June 1968 demonstrated a gap between an authoritarian President and an articulate section of the public across which nearly a century of republican government had failed to build a strong parliamentary bridge. Some commentators have noted the extinction of the strikes by material concessions, and the suppression of the student uprisings by 'firmness', and the routing of political opposition by an appeal to the fear of subversion and conspiracy; and have compared these setbacks to yet another defeat of the revolutionary movement that burst out in 1789, 1830, 1848 and 1871. Certainly the political gap left unfilled by Parliament was widely recognized. Not until May 1968 did Georges Pompidou, Prime Minister since 1962, act with publicly recognized authority in his own name; and he was quickly dropped by the President in June after the elections he had done much to win. And when in September 1968 M. Edgar Faure as Minister of National Education presented his university reform bill it was passed without any opposing votes although the left-wing parties could not have claimed that M. Faure's proposals measured up to their own manifestos. The gap between the political authority

TABLE 4. The thirteen universities of Paris

Paris I   *Major area of study: economics and law*
            Economics—public and administrative law—business law—
            international and European relations—philosophy of
            sciences—modern languages.
            * Possible co-operative programmes with the Institut
            d'Etudes Politiques.

Paris II   *Major area of study: law*
            Civil law—social psychology—applied computer science—
            French Institute of the Press—modern foreign languages.
            * Possible co-operative programmes with the Institut
            d'Etudes Politiques.

Paris III   *Major area of study: modern languages*
            Modern languages—school of interpreters—law—theatrical
            and cinematographic techniques of expression and com-
            munication.
            * Possible co-operative programmes with: Ecole Pratique
            des Hautes Etudes, Audio-visual Centre of Saint-Cloud,
            National Centre of Educational TV, Conservatoire
            National des Arts et Métiers—Conservatoire National d'Art
            Dramatique.

Paris IV   *Major area of study: classical studies*
            French language and literature—Latin—Greek—languages
            and civilizations of Eastern Europe—English, German
            and Spanish studies—applied sciences—computer science
            applied to linguistics—history of philosophy—aesthetics—
            medieval studies—applied literary and scientific studies.
            * Possible co-operative programmes with: Ecole Pratique
            des Hautes Etudes—Institut d'Etudes Politiques—Ecole
            des Chartes—Conservatoire de Musique—Ecole des
            Beaux-Arts.

Paris V   *Two major areas of study: medicine and human sciences*
            Medicine—human and experimental biology—dental sur-
            gery — pharmacy — legal medicine — psychology — social
            sciences—educational sciences—mathematics—formal logic
            and computer science—physical education—University
            Institute of Technology (information—statistical computer
            sciences—marketing).
            * Possible co-operative programmes with: Institut
            Pasteur—Museum of Natural History—Ecole Pratique
            des Hautes Etudes.

TABLE 4 (*continued*)

Paris VI	*Major area of study : sciences* Theoretical physics—physical chemistry—organic chemistry — physiology — earth sciences — mathematics — computer sciences and statistics—Institute of Programming—modern languages—geography (research).
Paris VII	*Interdisciplinary university par excellence* Medicine — biology — genetics — algebra and geometry — physics — chemistry — anthropology — human clinical sciences — geography — social sciences — English studies —sciences of texts and documents—linguistic research—sciences of religion. * Possible co-operative programme with: Ecole Pratique des Hautes Etudes—Museum of Natural History—Ecole Supérieure d'Electricité—Institut National Agronomique.
Paris VIII	Study and research unit (UER) of Vincennes Studies centred on contemporary problems—modern languages—human sciences.
Paris IX	*Study and research unit (UER) of Dauphiné* Management and applied economy (first cycle) — sciences of organization (third cycle)—computer sciences and management—Institute of Urbanism (will be ultimately transferred to Créteil)—applied economics—management (second cycle).
Paris X	*Study and research unit (UER) of Vincennes* Arts—law—University Institute of Technology of Ville-d'Avray (electronics and mechanics).
Paris XI	*Major area of study : sciences* Medical studies (first cycle)—biology (first cycle at Montrouge)—Institute of Nuclear Physics—University Institute of Cachan (chemistry, engineering, mechanics, electronics, computer science)—University Institute of Technology of Saclay-Orsay (chemistry) — juridical and economical sciences—therapeutic chemistry—environmental sciences. * Possible co-operative programmes with: Ecole Centrale des Arts et Manufactures—Ecole Supérieure de Chimie.
Paris XII	Medicine (at Créteil)—law and economics (at Saint-Maur)—ecology—medical computer sciences (second cycle)—Institute of Urbanism (subsequently).
Paris XIII	*Still incomplete* Law and economics (future University of Villetaneuse)—Arts and human sciences (Villetaneuse)—University Institutes of Saint-Denis, Villetaneuse, Argenteuil (still in project).

and an articulate but powerless section of the governed was recognized too by the President who promised 'participation' as one of the fruits of his future policy. Yet his own style of government had left little room for the expression of representatives' opinions. He had preferred either a physical, direct transmission of authority, or at least of support for his mission, by occasional contact with admiring crowds whose hands he touched; or the one-way transmission of his own decisions by television. When de Gaulle was abroad in Roumania, or on his return was keeping his silent counsel, the régime looked as if it must fall; the parliamentary majority seemed irrelevant if he were not actively leading. And when the President spoke out firmly on 30 May, refusing to resign and summoning the nation to order, the revolt began to subside.

Certainly, too, 'participation' was what students, *lycéens*, parents and workers wanted. The word is very ambiguous, and de Gaulle's mastery of ambiguity was well known. For him it almost certainly did not mean participation in the process of political decision-making or in the transmission of political authority between the governor and the governed. It could mean, as it probably did for the workers, a greater share in profits and in works councils. And for parents, teachers and students, a greater share in the membership of school councils and university committees. It seems unlikely, however, that the unions that tasted power would easily forget their successes. It is even more certain that students who have realized their own power as an indispensable élite will not be content with powerless participation, or will 'play the game' according to rules they did not write, or will be grateful for concessions when they feel that they can take whatever they want. The fragility of university and perhaps of parliamentary institutions has been demonstrated; and if the latter are not to be strengthened as the expression of opposition (and the opposition parties apparently did not even think it worth while to vote against the new majority in 1968) then the gap may well be crossed by the new power-making élite in the way that President de Gaulle bridged it occasionally: by direct contact between people and authority in the streets.

It has long been known that education and politics could not be kept apart; for governments provide the resources and to some extent direct policy. But now the action of the educated and the educands upon government has been shown to be strong, and even direct. The facts that the élite had no concerted policy and that students were surprised by the success of their newly discovered techniques prevented the movement from transcending protest to constitute an alternative claimant for power.

8

Educational planning within limits

The pressure to plan

The General Planning Commission has been responsible since 1946 for a succession of economic plans designed to improve the performance of the country. Since 1951 there has operated also a tributary commission for planning the development of France's education services. It is not difficult to see why they should be the subject of special surveys and forecasts. They are the largest public service. The budget for 1970 was 26·1 thousand million francs. The demands for manpower to staff the services rose constantly throughout these two decades since 1950. The decisions taken about the length of compulsory schooling and the size of the technical sector obviously affect the productive manpower of a nation, and are viewed in all modern economies as a form of investment in the nation's intellectual capital. Within the framework of this kind of thinking and of the nation's general plan, the education commission had to foresee its own investment needs, administrative measures and recruitment of personnel.

The French concept of planning is not that of total control. Of course forecasts are made as accurately as possible of the demand for schools, equipment and personnel, and of the developing change in the nation's manpower. Account is taken of industrialization and of urbanization, and of the need for a more mobile and adaptable labour force. And the country's need for a highly trained and intelligent élite is borne in mind too, so that the quality of advanced education is not damaged. So there is a conscious attempt to produce a plan and subsidiary plans that are generally consistent. For many years now this has implied an expansion of the education services. But some restraint on the expansion has been exercised almost every year as some of the budgetary allocations are withheld by the Ministry of Finance.

The expansion is, of course, competing with other claims upon the nation's resources. In the period of the Fourth Plan, educational investment enjoyed special priority, which in turn meant that the level of recurrent expenditure on education had to rise in the next period even though investment was slowed down to a rate more comparable with that of the government services. This competition is restrictive; but the fact is essential to the process of planning itself—limited resources are to be distributed to competing claimants.

Nor is the process totally 'centralized'. French planning refers to regions, and educational planning in particular makes demands upon *académies* and *départements*. This tendency to 'decentralize' is being encouraged. And the planning commissions include teachers' representatives as well as officials; consultation and persuasion were part of the concept of planning before the events of 1968 gave prominence to the term 'participation'. The planning function of the Ministry has been located at various points in the last decade; in 1963 it was established as one of the main services attached to the Secretary-General's office. The commission is not external to the Ministry. A fundamental principle of French planning, wrote M. Poignant, is that 'it is the normal role of a public administration worthy of its name to reflect upon its own development—on its constant adaptation to the evolution of society.' He went on to comment on the boundaries, or lack of them, between planning in advance and administrating within a general framework.

> However, planning is not only the work of conception, but even more the concrete business of execution extending throughout the development of the plan; the executive operations of successive plans fall to the Ministry of National Education and tend increasingly to merge with its ongoing activity.
>
> (Crémieux-Brilhac, 1965)

The majority of members constituting the commission are drawn from the branches and services within the Ministry; they are joined by representatives of other Ministries that control schools, by representatives of the Economic Council, of Higher Education, of employers and of teachers' unions, and of other commissions that contribute to the national plan. Their work is to estimate in some detail the foreseeable needs in terms of investment and personnel. These estimates are submitted for governmental approval and are considered in relation to the whole plan. Decision about the level of investments and the scale of recruitment is a political act. It is within the framework laid down by governmental decision that the educational equipment plans are subsequently implemented. Moreover, among the factors taken into account by the commission, in addition to demographic, social and economic pressures, is the enacted legislation about the extent of schooling and the structure of the educational system; and these are politically determined.

The Planning Commissions that operated up to 1970 were obliged to produce responses to immense demands. Their problems were demographic and quantitative—how to equip the education system with the buildings and staff that growing numbers of students demanded. The Fifth Plan (1966-9) was called the 'concrete plan' because of the concentration upon building. By the end of the decade the Minister had set up a computer programming division within the Ministry to assist with costing, with the calendar of decisions to be taken and with forecasts of the resources necessary to carry out each operation. A planning group within the Ministry was set to work on costs, and another one was commissioned to produce an outline of educational needs which the major commission for the Sixth Plan (1970-3) would use as guidelines. So at last a group was able to give attention to broad lines of development and to pedagogical problems.

The group recognized that the new plan would have to encourage innovation, and not just at the experimental level. Wide diffusion of new techniques would be required. The decade of pilot projects was over. Somehow, the children's experience of life and their experience of the classroom would have to be linked more closely. New motives would have to be discovered and used so that constraint and punishment might give way to the encouragement of curious, information-seeking, self-propelling young people who would learn how to find knowledge and how to use it. Clubs and societies would have to be multiplied. Planners now took account of qualitative growth.

New methods of teaching mathematics and languages would, it was hoped, affect the structure of the educational system. The too rigid distinction between scientific and literary pupils might, under new forms of tuition, give way to a distinction between abstract and concrete intelligences; and this in turn would affect the structure of secondary schools. The group agreed that the system at present offers a set of tracks that lead to success or inadequacy and elimination, and that the transition from one course to another is still so difficult as to be a source of frustration and failure. The new tasks call for more preparation of teachers in both practical and theoretical work. The group hoped that there would be no separation of various categories of teacher during the training period. New communication techniques did mean however that a clear distinction must now be made between the preparation of lessons—selection and grading of material—and their diffusion.

The transition of pupils from schooling to wage-earning occupied the attention of the working group. Family pressures and the desire for adult status was thought to be pushing young people too quickly into employment that might prove to be stunting; yet the young apprentice could be seen to be avid for vocational qualifications and forgetful of the general education he had undergone hitherto. So the school must introduce young people helpfully to the world of paid work, and the Sixth Plan must provide for an enormous increase in documentation for careers, in counsellors and in research into the sort of knowledge, aptitudes and adaptability that modern wage-earning requires.

The social aspects of education were also pointed out to the next commission. The social origins of students play less part than they did (in the universities 1·4 per cent of working-class sons were students in 1938, 5·3 per cent in 1959 and 9·4 per cent in 1965) in determining the chances of a higher education, but the position was still not satisfactory. Improvement might come from the merging of *collèges d'enseignement secondaire* with the new, more modest, *collèges d'enseignement général*, and from the coalescence of different types of curriculum. But more important would be forms of social assistance: more generous bursaries in secondary schools, free transport and school books, better canteen and hostel services. Within the schools the great need would be for more individualization of teaching, greater respect for a culture derived from concrete things and experiences rather than deduced from abstract principles, and the development of human qualities rather than skill in mental gymnastics.

Of course this kind of forward thinking can only be general and is bound to sound trite to those who have been familiar with the vocabulary of reform for some time. But the fact that pedagogical considerations have been offered to the commission (even before its members were nominated) is significant in the development of French planning. Certain qualities of education are being recommended, and the commission is being reminded that they must be planned for and paid for, just as the construction of schools had been.

The budget

The budget of the Ministry of National Education is not the only source of financial support for educational work in France. Other Ministries control their own enterprises; so do industrial firms; and so also do religious organizations. But the growth of the budget of the Ministry of National Education is indicative of the expansion that has taken place. It rose from 2·2 million francs in 1952 to 15·7 million francs in 1966. Had the value of the franc remained constant this would have represented a rise to 10·5 million francs or a multiplication by the factor 4·7. In terms of a percentage of the national revenue, the figure rose from 2 per cent to 4·6 per cent: and in terms of a percentage of the total government budget, from 7·2 per cent to over 16 per cent. (A. Garcia in Crémieux-Brilhac, 1965.)

The reasons for such a rapid rise are not difficult to find. First among them is the increase in the number of pupils and students, from approximately 5·2 million to 9·1 million, and connected with this response to the demand for education is the rising cost of providing better quality as well as greater quantity. As the wave of demographic growth has reached the primary, secondary and higher establishments in turn, these have expanded and improved their response. But the passage of the wave has not meant a subsequent reduction of costs in the primary or junior secondary sectors. A new classroom, new mathematical equipment, a new college of general education, a new corps of counsellors once supplied have to be maintained, even if the number of pupils in any one year drops slightly.

Moreover, the State has progressively extended the range of its financial responsibilities. The Marie law of 1951 made bursaries available to pupils in private schools. The Barangé law of the same year made State grants available for the improvement of salary scales in private schools. And, most importantly and controversially, the Debré law of 1959 made it possible for private schools to enter into contracts with the State in respect of certain classes and certain teachers whose costs the State would then take over.

A further factor has been the interpretation of 'democratization' to mean ease of access to school; this has meant the supply of free textbooks until the pupil reaches the end of the first secondary cycle, an increase in boarding accommodation and in bursary assistance to meet costs, more school meal services and an extension of the school bus services. In itself this latter service, combined as it is with the establishment of secondary schools in towns that serve a rural region, is bound to make young people more familiar with the towns and more dependent on urban services, and so to reinforce the drift of population from the villages. Yet village schools cannot be closed and their staffs transferred at a rate that would financially affect the cost of providing and staffing new primary schools and new colleges of secondary education. And in any case, the transformation of France into a nation with a modern agriculture and a modern industrial technology has meant the development of new schools, new institutes of technology and new research centres. This modernization is costly and the expensive items can be seen in the new academic university centres which will, it is hoped, strengthen the economies of the regions they serve. In so far as they do so, the budget is operating as a tool for redesigning the economic geography of France within the general framework of the series of plans.

The extent to which the budget activates planning is limited. Writing about the decade 1955–65, Majault says:

In fact, despite their growth and their relative importance, the budgets granted to National Education in the course of this decade have not been budgets of expansion but budgets of reception, measured to fit the emergencies. It is the same with the plans drawn up for the years to come within the Fifth Plan: whereas for example one forecasts 719,000 additional children in the pre-school system, only 343,000 places are to be provided: for the 561,000 pupils following the complete secondary course, 452,000 places are assured, and 688,000 for the full secondary cycle as against the 964,000 needed; in

higher education, 675,000 places are planned against the
792,000 judged to be necessary . . . Jules Ferry's golden rule,*
if adapted to the requirements of the close of this century,
would demand that $\frac{1}{6}$ or $\frac{1}{4}$ of the budget should be allocated to
education, if, in the words of the rapporteurs of the Plan, one
wanted to pass from passive planning, which simply aims to
meet the need as it develops, to active planning in which
educative activity is put at the service of a national design.

(Majault, 1967)

Although the share of the total national budget represented by the
Ministry's expenditure grew rapidly from 1960 to 1965 (i.e. from
11·87 to 16·35 per cent), thereafter the rate of growth slowed down
and in 1970 the share was about 17 per cent. The Minister (M.
Guichard in November 1969) accounted for this smaller growth by
referring to the smaller annual increase in the number of pupils and
students in this latest quinquennium. He hoped to improve the
'output of the machine' by administrative and pedagogical measures
such as programming, mechanized controls and avoiding any need
for pupils to retake the same class. The size of the budget excited
some Deputies in the National Assembly to expect efficiency and
return for money. Opposition Deputies saw this anxiety as a restraint upon future expansion and a postponement of that 'renewal'
that had so often been announced but hardly implemented. Political
pressures on the Minister to be efficient and to innovate are not
necessarily irreconcilable, for while reformers might not be too
happy with the thought of the educational system as a machine,
they do agree that machinery within the administrative offices can
contribute to the quality of planning.

On the other hand, those Deputies who stress 'return for money'
or 'efficient output' may be referring to a factor in planning that is
not necessarily consistent with the French commitment to democratization. There is great difficulty in assessing the value of the
system's output. Those who fail to complete courses they have
started at school or university may be cited as evidence of inefficiency
in the system, or of its generosity in offering each student a chance to
go as far as he can. France is now committed to an emphasis on
language and mathematics in the primary school; to a common

* That one-sixth of the national budget should be allocated to education.

trunk of education in the middle school; to non-selective entry into university for all who hold a *baccalauréat* or its equivalent; to various social measures (bursaries, free transport, etc.)—all of which are designed to make more equitable the pupils' chances of profiting from what is offered. It is assumed that an adequate élite will emerge from the mass and that specialized skills can best be acquired on a foundation of general education. So the planning is not for rigidity of social structure or of employment—or at least not for inflexible individuals within the structure. The belief in general education is consistent with the absence of detailed manpower planning by the educationists. Such inefficiencies as become apparent each year can be rectified within the four-year plan by the annual organization of the *rentrées*. So those who present the education system's needs for consideration by the General Planning Commission must defend a concept of planning and of social values. So far, this has apparently met with approval. But if the right-wing Deputies mean by 'efficiency' the allocation of resources to those classes or groups who might show the greatest benefit, then this could mean diverting resources to the least handicapped rather than to the socially under-privileged, and the process of democratization would be contested. Plans and budgets reflect certain social and cultural values.

The limits of bureaucracy

Pressure to reform the administration is beginning to come from parents too. The President of the Association of Parents of pupils in public schools said in a press interview in October 1969 that an essential reform was related to the administrative methods of the service. There was, he claimed, a lack of administrators trained to administer, and a special working party of civil servants should be formed with the task of getting the necessary reforms started. In his complaint he referred to secondary posts left unfilled in some places while teachers elsewhere were left without appointments. He suggested that teachers should know by July where they were to teach in the autumn, and that many more teachers should receive permanent appointments so that the supply of auxiliaries could be deployed more rapidly. And he recommended the use of computers.

There is no doubt that such immense operations as the autumn return to school (*la rentrée*) and the provision of classes and teachers are complicated and that the Ministry is not yet satisfied with its own information and planning services. The *recteur* of Paris reckoned that he was short of 800 teachers in September 1969. Teachers put the figure at 2,000. The shortage does affect the size of classes and the quality of teaching and is therefore relevant to the Minister's concern for renovation. Complexity and confusion also give added point to the Minister's intention to decentralize, starting in 1970 a pilot scheme for the reform of rectoral administration in the academic districts of Grenoble and Toulouse. Some indication of what is involved in central planning is offered by a circular issued in November 1969 in a further attempt by the Ministry to cope adequately with each succeeding *rentrée*.

Whereas the 'school map' is a projection drawn with a view to future age-groups, the growth of towns, the mobility of labour, the need to expand technical education and similar developments, the new 'basic map' will be drawn as a static interpretation of how things stand on a given date and it will be used as a planning tool for the next two years. Computer programmes will help to distribute resources more exactly to needy localities and to plan for the *rentrée* that lies nearly two years ahead. So the procedure inaugurated in November 1969 was in four phases. First came a critical examination of the situation in each school and the compilation of needs and of decisions to be taken centrally about co-education or optional subjects, or new syllabuses. Secondly, each locality would be told by 1 January what building would be carried out in readiness for September and what would be budgeted for in the next year. The Ministry and regional offices would also decide by 15 April what teachers and other staff would be required. Third, by 1 July the central administration would have taken the particular decisions about appointments and allocation of funds, and would have completed examinations and promotions in the higher education sector. Fourth, by mid-August all teachers would have been posted.

The amount of decisions to be taken centrally and their dovetailing into those that can be made regionally constitute huge tasks. It is little wonder that the Minister wants to decentralize and to call on the aid of computers for this administrative work. These two measures may leave him and some of his staff more free to consider the major problems of policy that are a particular source of disruption in the State.

The organs of the commission within the Ministry are expected to estimate and recommend the amount of investment in national education, and to indicate the necessary financial and administrative measures. As far as actual decisions about investments, building sites and operations are concerned, the commission itself takes responsibility for higher education. It delegates to other administrative services, and to other national or local authorities the design of the *carte scolaire*, i.e. the detailed recommendations about the development of primary and secondary schooling. The drafting of the *carte scolaire* will be referred to in a later chapter concerned with the economic and social environment of educational services. The forecasting of students' needs and the planning of new university structures will be examined in the section dealing with educational problems in relation to institutions. Meantime, we can record that men of intelligence and some foresight, equipped with organs of information such as the *Bureau Universitaire de Statistique*, strive to co-ordinate schools, budgets, manpower needs and political legislation. The location of new universities and of new secondary schools has some effect on the geography of the country and creates new centres of social activity which may some day acquire powers if a policy of decentralization is really pursued. The commission can claim considerable success in recruiting teachers of various qualifications. And the commission will also be blamed for failing to foresee or to persuade the government to anticipate extensive unrest in universities and schools. The grounds of the discontent included resentment about lack of buildings and staff, restriction of visits between men and women, anxiety about employment after graduation and, paradoxically, the assumption that students were just manpower to service the economy. All these are factors in planning, and the 1968 riots seem to indicate that the planners had not attributed the correct weight to them.

An interviewer (M. Girod de l'Ain of *Le Monde*) suggested to the Minister in 1969 that while the number of pupils and teachers had doubled in fifteen years the organization of the Ministry remained much the same. He cited the absence of forecasts and of information on decisions taken, and he suggested that several Ministers had wanted a functional organization of the Ministry into sections, each responsible for a single task, such as the training of teachers. The Minister admitted that the recent elimination of the Secretary-General's office had not been very well thought out and had left some unsolved problems. Two principles would guide future reorganization: maximum decentralization and the use of computer programming to supply information about budgets and tasks. The Minister also said that one should not touch the wheels of a machine before knowing how it works and that he was still at the stage of observation and analysis. This is, no doubt, a prudent comment. But in view of the rapidity with which Ministers succeed each other in a post which few of them have actively sought, such restraint must operate also as a brake upon reform. It adds weight also to the suggestion that a working party should be released from other duties in order to bring the Ministry up-to-date.

PART THREE

Educational problems

9

Points of transition

Entry into secondary courses

In a system characterized by the assumption that a pupil of a certain age will be in a certain numbered class in the series and will be able to cope with the work set in the written syllabus for that year, it is normal to view the transition from one class to another as a reasonable step up the ladder of knowledge. So a pupil could reasonably be admitted to the *classe de sixième* in a secondary school if he had shown by his performance that he was equipped to do the work of that class. This was the assumption underlying the entry examination that was replaced in 1960 (except for pupils coming from private elementary schools, and for those whose work record did not justify the transition) by record cards and teachers' assessments. But the structure—the syllabus for each class, and the transfer from the primary class with its one teacher, to the secondary school with its subject specialists, its claim to culture and its vistas of higher education—remained the same. The gap was large, and the legitimacy of the difference between the two forms of schooling was, for Frenchmen, reinforced by Piaget's findings about the development of the child's mind from concrete to formal operations, and by Wallon's belief that an eleven-year-old child knows himself to be a multiple personality playing different roles in different groups (Reuchlin, 1966).

Despite the structural changes effected in the last decade, the passage from primary school to secondary school is hardly yet a simple step from one rung to another. A record book for continuous observation and guidance was made available to primary schools in 1960. Information was to be inscribed about the pupil's backgrounds—family, professional, cultural and psychological, about his health, his nursery school record, the character traits observed in class; his annual letter of general assessment (A, B+, B, B— or C), and his awakening interests. A tool of this kind has to be used, and the comment of M. Roger Gal in 1965 was discouraging.

We are not sure that the possible uses of this dossier have been fully understood and explained and we fear that, in the absence of precise initiation, this instrument has seemed to many to be 'just one more piece of paper' to be filled in, whereas really the future of the child is at stake.

The inflexibility of teachers' habits is matched by the syllabuses that seem to have been designed for the fast learners. Basic concepts such as the relationship of subject and complement in a sentence, or the addition and subtraction of fractions in arithmetic, were shown by investigators to have been very inadequately understood. At the age of nine, a third of the children were already a year behind. Either the secondary school programme was excessive in its demands, or the teaching methods were failing to overcome social and cultural handicaps in the pupils. Certainly the passage from primary to secondary school was shown to be a large gap to be jumped rather than a normal step to be taken. Here lay a crucial structure. Greater concentration on basic mechanisms of languages and of counting, a slower pace to ensure thorough familiarity with operations before swift manipulation of derived concepts is required; these were pedagogical problems whose solution demanded the careful training and encouragement of primary school teachers free from the pressure of a secondary school syllabus.

Until this kind of reform is achieved, the secondary school must be organized to cope with the teaching that has not been completed in this primary school. So differentiation of streams or sections must characterize the secondary school, and the classification of pupils enters too soon into operations that should postpone it until the end of a four-year cycle. Such classification is precarious as well as precocious. According to an investigation carried out between 1962 and 1965 in the department of Eure (Normandy), primary teachers assessed their pupils more severely in French than in arithmetic with the result that rural pupils from verbally poor backgrounds were penalized; young rural teachers (who will be drawn into towns as their career progresses) were anyway very uncertain in their assessments; and a quarter of the pupils scored unevenly in their performance in these two fields, being strong in one and weak in the other. Yet pupils tended to be grouped in classes according to general ability: those whose future included a study of Latin being younger and verbally brighter as opposed to those who were older, who came from poorer families and who performed less well in verbal tests. Four years later the two groups were identifiable also by their aspirations at the end of the orientation cycle. The postponement of Latin (in 1968) from the curriculum of the first two years may not have eliminated this sort of perpetuated classification, for the *classe de sixième* in some *lyceés* still is divided into two sections one of which is young and fast. The influence of the *agrégés*, fighting a rearguard action in favour of the early recognition of quality against M. Faure's attempt to establish a *tronc commun*, is said to be reflected in this practice. And in 1970 Latin was re-introduced into class five as part of their French syllabus.

The difference between pupils entering a *lycée* and those entering a college of general education in 1960 was not in the amount of knowledge they brought with them. The latter were about a year older. Entry still was largely influenced by the background and aspirations of parents. Research workers foresaw a long task ahead of the information and guidance services—perhaps the work of a whole generation before orientation would be given and accepted mainly on pedagogical grounds. The research service of the *Institut Pédagogique National* asked (in 1965) for an experimental college of secondary education, alleging that research at the level of the observation cycle was not yet experimental in the proper sense of the term. Such a college would require a well-trained volunteer corps of teachers anxious to experiment. Even the *lycées pilotes* never achieved that, for although the *proviseur* of such a school might hope that teachers promoted to his staff would enter into 'the spirit of the school' there was no guarantee that any new teacher would share his enthusiasm; and there is no pressure that can compel an uninterested teacher to adopt new practices.

Instructions issued in 1960 for the guidance of those teachers who would be concerned with the observation cycle advised them to look out for the potential and special nature of the pupil's intelligence. They stressed the importance of identifying those children whose skill in syntactical analysis marked them out as future Latinists; for they were to be put to their Latin in the second term of secondary schooling, according to the original reform of 1959. The teacher exercising his new function as an adviser was requiring not only to mark grammatical exercises, as in the past, but also to interpret the mark as an indication of the pupil's potential gift for dealing in abstractions, for discovery, for reasoning and for disentangling problems. The problems might be mathematical or scientific in fact, but the instructions gave no examples of these and concentrated on demonstrating how the nature of a grammatically complex sentence might exercise and reveal the pupil's intelligence. Although reformers had already won recognition in principle for environmental studies, for art and craft and music, for crossing subject barriers so that a language lesson might bring in any light shed by history and geography, yet the instructions referred to none of these.

Easing the passage

The necessary reform in the primary school, which would permit the liberation of progressive secondary teachers, was announced late in 1969 following the report of a ministerial commission on the renewal of primary education.

The commission made the following points. Extension of schooling has changed the goal of the elementary school; it is now, for all pupils, a preparatory institution leading to secondary studies. Yet its function may well be to prolong the work of the infant school and nursery schools, rather than to anticipate the later stage. The primary school must not look too far ahead lest distant objectives distort its own function. It is to provide for development, not for training.

So the primary school will take into account the biological and psychological needs of the children. It will provide time for three kinds of activity: artistic expression and stimulation, physical education and games, and work in language and mathematics. Within this triple division of time, one half will be devoted to language and mathematics, and these activities will take place in the morning as being the period when pupils are freshest. The transmission of knowledge is to give place to the development of aptitudes, habits and attitudes. Less reference will be made to books and more to 'modern life itself'. The aim is to provide the children with techniques for finding out, for expression and communication. Relationships between teacher and pupil are to be characterized by 'democratic' dialogue. Pupils are to be co-operative rather than competitive among themselves. And teachers are to collaborate with colleagues, parents and youth leaders.

The commission emphasized the hope that division of the day into 'triple time' would not mean exclusive treatment of subjects in each period, and would not suggest that some activities taught techniques while others developed personality. Judgment, sensitivity and physical skills enter into the work of mastering language and number.

The commission drew attention to a major weakness in the French schools: the number of those pupils who have to repeat a class. The commission called for an end to this phenomenon. In turn this means that the work of each class year can no longer be based on a composite syllabus combined with several subjects and on the promotion of those pupils who achieve a satisfactory general average score. So there will have to be groups or sets in language and in mathematics, each set working at its own pace and level. There can, then, be no yearly syllabus of work to be got through.

Two further changes follow. Each form-teacher will keep his or her pupils for at least two years, starting with the nursery schools, so that the teacher in charge of the five-year-olds will accompany them up into the first year of the primary school. And teamwork among teachers will be necessary to ensure that all information is passed on from one teacher to the next. The demands to be made on teachers would be severe. Not only must they be expert in language and number, but as form-teachers they will be expected to encourage, demonstrate and take part in much of the physical and artistic education as well as in environmental studies. Obviously, their training as teachers will have to be many-sided and continuous.

The new organization of the school day and the principles enunciated by the commission were accepted by the Minister and now have to be turned into factual reform in this decade. He himself foresees difficulties. The priority in the teaching process is to pass from the material to the pupil—but teachers are proud of their knowledge and anxious to display and transmit it. Reference is to be made to the environment rather than to books—but the textbook has always been a major instrument shaping the course of the lesson and offering a methodology. The school's new attitude is expressed in terms such as 'stimulus', 'awakening', 'arousal'—but many teachers think of work as hard grind and see the children as vessels to be filled rather than as organisms to be motivated. The teachers' working day will be reduced by one hour—but the obligation upon them to use this hour for their own retraining (probably in association with a radio programme) is only a moral one. More serious efforts at in-service training would, the Minister recognized, have to be made by freeing them for courses lasting three months. The Minister claimed that retraining would affect all teachers: the period of pilot-projects was over.

In effect these new proposals remove some of the hardship and awkwardness from points of transition by blurring the hitherto acutely clear boundaries between one level of education and the next. If this new spirit of education prevails in the primary school it may spread upwards into the colleges of general and of secondary education where many teachers work who formerly were attached to the 'primary sector'. Their cycle of studies is now a 'common trunk' for at least two years; and the pupils may not leave for another two years; so the pressure of marks, promotion or choice of employment need not be great, and the boundary between the primary and the secondary schools may in turn lose its formidability. But changes in attitudes take time, and psychological barriers resulting from the widely held belief in the superiority of traditional secondary general education still prevents the system from adopting the best that primary or technical schools can demonstrate. We meet this barrier again in the difficulty that successive Ministers have lamented in trying to encourage more pupils to cross over into the technical sector.

The middle school under stress

The concept of the 'middle school' has gained increasing acceptance since it was first debated and rejected in 1957. Two years later M. Berthoin launched, rather timidly, the process of reform that can still be restrained but apparently not arrested. His 'observation cycle' for the first two years of secondary schooling was a very moderate proposal, designed to open the flood-gates only a little wider in response to demographic and social pressures. His observation cycle was to be a period during which the syllabuses of various kinds of secondary school were to be 'harmonized' as far as possible so that teachers and parents could discern the true aptitudes of pupils and take appropriate decisions about their next cycle of studies. The brilliant pupils could start Latin in the second term of the first year, and the dull pupils who still had some elementary knowledge to acquire remained in *classes de fin d'études* which were primary in nature and affiliation. Nor did the observation cycle constitute an indisputable part of the secondary sector; each cycle in each different type of school was staffed and administered by the educational branch—primary, secondary or technical—to which the school as a whole belonged.

Nevertheless, the reform contained seeds of growth that could not be impeded. Advice about pupils' further studies was given by a 'guidance council' of teachers; this implied both the keeping of records (not just marks) and the co-operation of teachers as teams. The teaching of some secondary school subjects in schools affiliated to the primary sector meant that *professeurs* had to be borrowed or transferred, and that *instituteurs* could prepare themselves for upgrading by in-service study and training; so barriers became less impermeable. A corps of special advisers or counsellors was established; their growth was slow but the concept of educational guidance by those who had special training in educational psychology and in vocational guidance introduced a new category of professional educator into a system that could not easily accommodate it. And within the schools, those teachers concerned with guidance also received some special preparation; so that the former traditional qualifications of a teacher in pedagogical method and subject mastery was shown to be incomplete. Gradually throughout the decade the inadequacy and also the growing power of these measures became evident, and the movement towards a common trunk of studies for at least two years and towards a four-year cycle of studies that would be 'autonomous' and separate from the *lycées* in which it was housed gave a new shape to the structure of secondary education. 'Observation' gave way to 'orientation'; and the cycle stretched from two to four years. In the process certain strains became evident. Their alleviation will take time.

The observation cycle was from the start subject to the strains felt by the type of school in which it was located. The Billères Bill had proposed intermediate schools which would not have been attached to any of the traditional branches of the Ministry, and in fact the development of the observation period into a four-year cycle of studies has partially fulfilled that proposal. Changes brought about in the Ministry in 1961 tended to co-ordinate various aspects of the administration of the observation cycle. Then the creation in 1963 of new colleges of secondary education prepared the way for an autonomous 'middle school'. In 1968 there were 1,500 such colleges in operation, and it was estimated that another decade would be needed in which to build all that was required. The ideal would be an establishment offering remedial or intensive teaching in transitional classes for the pupils who still were not skilled enough in language and number, a general course of studies as now offered in a college of general education and two courses of secondary studies for those who expected or aspired to continue their studies in the second cycle. Such a school would presumably benefit from flexible internal arrangements so that the practical work and special methods of the transitional classes would stimulate the more traditional teachers, and the specialist knowledge of the highly qualified would be available in various sections of the school, and transfer from one section to another would not be difficult. The decision taken by M. Faure in 1968 to postpone the learning of Latin so that the first two years could be organized round a really common bank of knowledge was a further step towards harmonization, and towards implementing the concept of a cycle.

The practice of promoting pupils from class to class, thanks to an average mark of ten or more, has been abandoned in favour of the guided passage of pupils from one cycle of studies to the next. The concept of the cycle—in 1959 it was only a two-year observation cycle, but it has gradually grown into the 'first' cycle of four years in a secondary school—has been extrapolated. Admission to a cycle of studies implies recognition that a pupil or student is fit to pursue the course and stands a good chance of gaining whatever qualification it leads to. Orientation consists in guiding the pupil into the appropriate course or stream of studies and in guiding him helpfully into another activity if the original estimate of his capacities proves wrong. The geographical location of these first cycles in colleges of secondary education was designed in 1963 to facilitate orientation. It was presumed that the assembling of different styles of course within one school would help teachers to detect pupils' abilities and to guide the pupils into 'transition classes' taught by a skilled and innovating *instituteur*, or into a short 'modern' course, or into a longer modern or classical course for those who took easily to verbal and abstract thought. While the Ministry's circulars were proposing these categories of class, the reformers were already asking for regrouping of pupils so that the more gifted could do more advanced study and research in the library while slower learners had more teaching in basic subjects. It was realized that any system of classes that would really offer comparable chances of success and not simply conform the selective factors at work in the primary school, would depend on skilled teaching. So the structured solution revealed more pressingly two pedagogical problems: the internal structure of the school, and the teaching methods employed in each section. The official text (21 April 1964) explaining the operation of the orientation councils of teachers, also admitted that although all pupils were entitled to a place in that second cycle to which the council had recommended them, it would be some time before enough technical establishments were available.

Just as some university students were anxious about the directive claims of the National Plan and others about its inefficacy, so too parents and educators are divided with regard to orientation. The educational ideal is the discovery of means whereby each young person is to realize himself fully. The economists recommend a rise in the numbers studying science and technology. The two views may not in the long run be irreconcilable, since the full development of the person usually implies his useful employment in the nation. But to attempt a reconciliation too early in the pupil's school career may be both to distort his inclination and to deprive him of that general education which will ensure later flexibility and adaptability. It is for this reason that the orientation cycle has been developed into four years of general education with as great a common core of studies in different sections of the CES as the professional resources are able or willing to provide. In large measure, however, this dynamic interpretation of the orientation cycle represents a normative myth rather than a present reality, and this is not only because the tasks of discovery and of counselling are entrusted to teachers who have received no special training in orientation.

The colleges of secondary education, of which there were 1,500 by the end of 1968 (including some enlarged and promoted colleges of general education) are being rapidly built but it will be many years before all the colleges of general education (except in isolated mountain districts) are absorbed into colleges of secondary education and all the *lyceés* transform their first cycle of studies into semi-autonomous multilateral middle schools. The professional obstacles in the path of this transformation have been mentioned in a previous chapter, and may be briefly recalled. The college of secondary education contains four different sections taught by different grades of teacher. The *agrégés* with highly specialized university qualifications now tend to cluster in the *lycée* proper, that is in the second cycle; but there are not enough of them. The university graduates with a year's additional training at a Regional Teaching Centre and a competitively won certificate teach mostly in the first cycle but aspire to the *lycée*. The primary *instituteur* who has gained his certificate of fitness to teach in a college of general education, having as qualifications his *baccalauréat* and part of the university course leading to a *licence*, teaches several subjects and claims that all pupils in at least the first two years of secondary school ought to be taught by his kind. And the university *licencié* with no additional training fills the many gaps, as an unestablished unattached teacher, paid less because not fully qualified, and usefully mobile because not appointed to the permanent teaching strength of any district. The really interesting new teaching is done in the transition classes which gradually replace the blatantly primary *classes de fin d'études primaires*—which, however, still took in 250,000 pupils in 1966. The transition class teachers can, by concentration on basic subjects and by work in small groups and by practical methods, bring on the slower learners to a point where, at the end of the first cycle, some clear orientation into work or into further study can be offered.

The new middle school has more problems than the competition between grades of teacher for status and classes. The co-existence of different traditions of teaching within one building does not mean that these will continue to flourish. A school which was highly regarded as a *cours complémentaire* prior to 1959, and was still recognizable locally as a college of general education until 1963, may not thrive or enjoy parents' confidence as a section of a college of secondary education in which preparation for industry or commerce is less valued than studies leading to the *baccalauréat*. And the corps of teachers who developed successful *cours complémentaires* is being diluted by the entry of teachers who have not been trained in the *écoles normales*. For the purposes of administration and remuneration, this corps of teachers in the multilateral school is supervised by inspectors of the primary system. The school as a whole is advised by more specialist inspectors who have less pedagogical aid to offer.

Those who uphold that form of excellence which the *lycée* promoted are apprehensive lest specialist studies be introduced in the first cycle by teachers whose own study of the subject was not deep enough to offer an exciting exploration. Specialism without the scholarship that leads to *culture générale* may be neither one form of excellence nor the other. And some *agrégés* deplore the loss of their younger pupils both because beginners should be taught by experts and because teachers find young pupils so refreshing.

Apprehensions of these kinds, about the loss of a traditional excellence or of a status, reflect the juxtaposition in one new form of several distinct institutions. The hope was, and still is, that fusion will take place and that flexibility will replace separateness, to the benefit of all pupils. This is not yet discernible outside a few pilot schools that have overridden the hourly divisions of the timetable, have built workrooms, classrooms, projection rooms, reading rooms and common rooms of different sizes and for both heterogeneous and homogeneous groups. Juxtaposition by itself does not bring down institutional partitions. New concepts of the timetable, of the teaching group and of teachers' preparation are needed too. Such observations lead us into some consideration of the pedagogical problems associated with reform.

The difficulties experienced in the colleges of secondary education have not so much daunted reformers as sharpened the issues that next engage attention. These were identified by the Secondary School Teachers' Union (SNES) in its Congress at Easter 1968. In outline, the colleges would consist of an observation period lasting two years, and a similar period for tentative orientation. At all stages the chance of catching up again must be offered to those who have fallen behind, and for those who do not continue their general studies beyond this first cycle, vocational education under the aegis of the Ministry of National Education (as opposed to private firms or some other Ministry) is demanded.

Both quantity and quality would have to rise: quantity because in the year 1966–7 only 512,000 pupils (in both public and private schools) were admitted to a truly secondary course (*lycée*, or CES or CEG), leaving 250,000 to enter a *classe de fin d'études primaires*; and quality because the growing diversity of needs to be met require new skills in the teachers, and new acceptance in secondary schools of artistic and physical education.

The new skills would include manipulation of a class or of classes in rearranged groups, and the ability to work with colleagues in a team. The concept of 'long' and 'short' courses will have to be abandoned so that the schools can be organized in groups moving at different rates, with transitional classes between the first three years. For the rapid learners special activities will be organized in addition to normal classes. Two of the Union's requests were met a few months later when M. Faure postponed the introduction of Latin for two years, and welcomed the teaching of technology in the third and fourth years. A third request—for participation by parents in the administration of the schools—was out of date by the time it was published. Before the end of the summer both parents and pupils were admitted to membership of the administrative councils.

There still remains to be tackled the task of educating all teachers up to the level of a post-university certificate and of introducing them to educational psychology, sociology and 'activity methods'. Structural reform has provided opportunities, but if they are to be exploited attention must now be given to the personal equipment of the teachers who work in the new structure; and this will be a task demanding even more sensitivity and time.

Relationships with technical institutions

The barriers to be broken down between institutions are, as we have seen, only partially those set up by syllabuses and administrative partitions. Prejudices, social habits, traditional concepts of hierarchy in schools and in industry still keep down the number of pupils opting to study for a technician's qualification. The country's developing industries need the technicians; but the reforms in education have not altered the habits of parents choosing their offspring's course of study. A general education leading to secure, if minor, posts in the railways or post office, or to teacher training, or to industrial or commercial work for which short specific training is given, is preferred to an outright decision to embark on a technical course. Nor does planning exert the pressure some would like to see if the needs of industry are to be met.

The Ministry's report for the year 1966 examined the situation and observed that a third of young people leaving school took jobs without having received any training; that training for girls was especially deficient; that jobs were lacking for those pupils who had taken the longer secondary course of technical studies and even more so for young semi-skilled and skilled workers: and that the numbers of those undergoing in-service training or professional upgrading should be doubled or tripled.

> The cause of these gaps and distortions [said the report] lies in
> the general organization of education which, until the reform of
> 1959, possessed a uniform and selective structure and school
> methods steeped in tradition. They have also resulted from the
> fact that the curricula and methods of technical education have
> not been adapted to its own purposes. Moreover, the great
> number of authorities acting in matters of education and
> vocational training, and out-moded and ill-adapted regulations
> have brought about a somewhat chaotic situation. Lastly,
> advancement and in-service training activities for adults have
> not been received with favour by the universities.

The report then referred to the reforms of 1966: new opportunities for positive guidance at the end of each stage of vocational studies; variety of courses in the colleges of secondary education; vocational certificates offered at the end of the short (two-year) upper secondary course; a technician's *baccalauréat*; the university institutes of technology; and the integration of school perspectives and vocational perspectives thanks to the guidance organization. Close co-operation was foreseen between public authorities and firms.

Such reforms represent, as always, some practical steps in the necessary direction and a measure of intention which it will take years to implement. Two years later M. Faure confessed that at least one aspect of co-operation had broken down: the transfer of fifteen-year-old pupils to part-time employment (because the schools were still not ready in 1967 to retain them all until the decreed age of sixteen years) had not proved successful. It is doubtful too whether the base of the reform was yet firmly enough established to support technical developments in the higher classes, for in 1966 over 650,000 'secondary' pupils were still reported to be in *classes de fins d'études primaires* which still belong administratively to the primary schools and are only gradually being transformed into 'transition classes' of the secondary school system. It is easier to decree a reform than to change the nature of a section of the system or of a section of the pupils.

The *lycée technique*, reduced really to the upper cycle of secondary studies (since the teaching of technology starts in the first cycle of the colleges of secondary education, and the new institutes take over again three years later), feels itself to be hard done by.

> Scarcely recovered from the amputations at its base and its summit, struck by a disquieting decrease in its numbers, paralysed by a sort of descending rigidity, still isolated in respect of the structures, procedures and administrative regulations, little sought after by professeurs and administrators, having only a handful of agrégés at its disposal, cruelly short of specialised teachers, still badly known, it (technical education) questions itself in a sort of sad resignation.
>
> (Baron, 1968)

The decline in quality and quantity of which M. Baron complained here may be due in part to the delay in teaching new industrial techniques and in part to the need for a basic general education built round French, mathematics and natural sciences. Such a foundation would be appropriate for all pupils in the second cycle, with varying emphasis, and the common curriculum would help to overcome the partitions between classical, modern and technical sections.

M. Faure claimed to be moving in that direction. But it is disappointing to read (in his speech to the National Assembly in November 1968) how he interpreted this development of technical education.

> First, it is necessary to open technology to all pupils, and we shall do it from the third year (*la quatrième*) on . . . All

pupils ought to know technology, for it is not unworthy of
intelligence . . . All pupils must get into the habit of taking up
some activity or other—they can choose—in which manual
work is present, such as drawing, book-binding, etc. Typical
training ought to be based on four years of general education,
on two years of technical college leading them to a technical or
vocational certificate, or to the two years of a so-called
technical *lycée*—which is really a *lycée* in which a technical
branch will have been developed . . . This scheme is not bad,
but as it stands, it cannot be realized yet.

The chief reason why it could not be implemented was given as the
need for remedial work with so many children who would, in time,
be those on whom technical education would draw. Meantime, said
M. Faure, the gangways between general and technical education
must be kept open. It sounds discouragingly reminiscent of M.
Berthoin's initial steps in 1959. The Minister then went on to
complain of the shortage of technical students in the science
faculties, and to persuade the Assembly that Latin was not a necessary component of a noble education in the schools and could be
postponed for two years.

One wonders whether such persuasive action will be effective in
the absence of the more complete implementation of those reforms
which would tend to delay for a few more years the almost definitive
decision about which school, that is which branch of the system and
which level of the hierarchy, the pupil will try to enter. The more
radical reformers, at least, deplore the slow rate of progress towards
an 'autonomous cycle', and they express serious doubts as to whether
any firm 'aptitudes' can be discovered at so early an age. Aptitudes,
they say, are flexible, changeable, indeterminate. A colloquium held
at Sèvres in 1963 gave up the attempt to list criteria by which a
pupil's success in classical studies might be predicted; the criteria
were found to be those on which future success as a technician was
also probable.

Colleges of technical education continue to increase in numbers.
They received in the academic year 1969/70 over half a million
students, which was 43,000 more than in the previous year. The
courses lead to certificates graded according to the number of years
of study required. Yet the number of students and the variety of

qualifications are still not satisfactory. Technical education is still not attractive enough to invite large numbers of young people to cross the frontier that separates it from the more reputable general education. To close the gap is a major purpose of policy.

The difficulties are great. From each age-cohort of 800,000 young people, 500,000 go as soon as possible into wage-earning or apprenticeship or into the short courses of study that succeed the first cycle. A good variety of courses must be offered if they are to acquire some qualification, be employable, fit the needs of the economy and yet not reach the end of their possible development and adaptability. The right kind of education would provide skills and a general basis of knowledge on which to build, and a taste for further learning. In other words, much of the education given in technical colleges must be recognizably 'general', just as the general education offered elsewhere should in principle contain a measure of technical skills. If the gap between the two were diminished, then parents might be less averse to sending their children into technical education. Meantime, the transition remains uninviting, and presents a major restraint upon the desired development of the education system and the economy.

10

Curriculum and teacher education

The syllabus and the child

For some observers, such as M. Louis Legrand (1963), the most pressing of reforms to be undertaken is the adaptation of the curriculum to the needs of the children. M. Legrand defended his proposition against those who contended that large classes were the chief obstacle to pupils' progress, by showing that the number of slow learners in primary schools was greater in rural districts despite smaller classes, than in towns, and that the number of slow learners in Geneva was smaller than in comparable French towns despite the similar size of classes. In his opinion, backed by reference to the research work of the *Institut Pédagogique National*, the principal causes of backwardness in school work were the linguistic poverty of the pupils' family and environment, and the dearth of affection that would offer the child an adequate sense of security. If, as M. Legrand wrote, more than half the primary pupils in some schools failed to reach the secondary stage without having repeated some section of the primary course, the fault lay less with the size of classes than with other factors which failed to compensate for or even fortified the influence of a verbally dull environment, viz. the spirit and content of the syllabus. Each syllabus seemed in fact to be designed and taught for the swiftly progressing group that throve in a verbal and abstract curriculum and graduated happily into the university preparatory course of a *lycée*. Unwillingness to recognize the need for adaptation of matter and method had bred in many teachers a belief in the 'pedagogy of effort'—if the child did not succeed he must try harder, and especially try to remember.

Rural teachers have felt hesitation about encouraging their pupils to aim for the *classe de sixième* in a *lycée*, and although more than two-thirds of the pupils leaving primary school now, since 1968, enter a two-year cycle which is supposed to be common to all students, yet the style and the assumptions of teachers are marked by their institutional background, and true orientation or guidance is frustrated because the most obvious measure of a pupil's capacity is his ability to cope satisfactorily with a mass of material to be absorbed, remembered and recalled, and with a style of presentation that relies on abstractions and symbols. The outcome in some villages is the group of youths who had hope and sparkle, but have failed in the secondary course of studies, and have lost their drive but cannot reconcile themselves to settling back into the village life they expected to put behind them.

Of those pupils who entered the *lycée* and stayed the full course to the *baccalauréat*, M. René Bazin calculated (1963) that only a quarter reached the examination within the supposedly normal seven years; which indicates that the syllabus and pace are adapted to the over-gifted. The modification of school organization from a ladder of classes, in which each rung was mounted only by those with a general average of ten marks out of twenty, to a series of cycles with no internal obstacles, has offered the necessary structural change. The end of each cycle gives teachers and pupils the chance to take stock and to determine in general terms whether the pupil continues his general education in the next cycle of studies or whether he follows one of the distributaries that lead to a technical or vocational qualification. How authentic this opportunity is, depends now on how enriching, stimulating, cultivating and educative the work of the cycle has been. The suitability of the material and the skills of the teachers are the important factors, and of course the Minister has always recognized this—in principle. Addressing the National Assembly in November 1963, M. Fouchet, regretting the past miscalculations of the Le Gorgeu Commission with regard to equipment and buildings, said, 'But buildings we always get in the end, even if it takes time, money, perseverance. The important thing, the essential thing, is what happens inside, is the great pedagogical reform.'

A few months previously, one of the Minister's Directors of Education responsible for secondary schooling, M. Haby, treated a gathering at Sèvres to another of those lucid analyses which demonstrate that the civil servants are fully aware of their problem but cannot guarantee from the government the necessary power to solve it or to alter its terms. Moral education he entrusted to a 'slow, progressive impregnation', assuming that the values of civilization tacitly underlay school life and that the models of man and societies set forth in school extracts from literature would enter the subconscious of the pupils.

> We also seek to make acceptable certain hierarchies of intellectual qualities: on the highest level we put logic, facility in abstraction, clarity of mind; we also give great weight to memory or to industrious work—much more than to imagination or sensitivity.

He went on to show the inadequacy of this too intellectual approach and the need to teach responsibility, imagination and initiative. He referred to the 'psychosis of failure, emphasized by the hierarchy of marks and of classifications or of examination placements' and to the need to teach judgment, a taste for creation and for reading, the art of living. Since secondary schooling was now the basic training for all future workers and mothers, as well as for managers, 'its traditional content cannot fail to be turned upside down.' Communication as a tool of human and professional contact has now to receive priority, and then the pupils must learn the techniques of different activities, and of analysis and synthesis in concrete situations. Reflection is to be encouraged rather than memorization. The amount of knowledge required should be greatly reduced, although the 'gymnastics of the mind' can only be exercised if some material has been committed to memory. The encyclopaedism of the syllabus, for too long an imitation of university requirements, is admitted, and the amount of material to be acquired by a pupil should be limited to the 'pegs' on which to hang an argument or an intellectual exercise. Apprenticeship for social life should be developed through extra-curricular clubs and activities, and elected pupils might even have administrative tasks in the school; this would give practice in operating the apparatus of a modern state.

The Director concluded by saying:

> Yes, I know that these personal reflections—which do not commit anybody except myself—have passed lightly over the psychological obstacles, the material limitations, the difficulties of implementation. Should I on that account have abstained from expressing them? In this field of education, which is both agonizing and stimulating, must one not sometimes rise with the wings of Icarus as if they would never melt?

Two observations will spring to the reader's mind at once. The first must be the Ministry's serious underestimation of the pupils' desire for real participation in the functioning of a public enterprise. The second is the perhaps too ready recognition of the gap between the desirable and the possible, although the bridging of this gap is in fact the politician's task.

The Minister attempted in May 1965 to draw the consequences of his own repeated assertion that 'all our educational structures have burst.' The new colleges of secondary education had been established two years before, so that all pupils would in time enter a four-year secondary cycle of studies even though these were still organized in four distinct streams, and the Minister now turned his attention to the second cycle of studies leading in three years to the *baccalauréat* examination. The new design appears in the diagram on pages 22 and 32. The main innovations were the introduction of economics with statistics to be studied along with Latin or a modern language; the opening of the modern side to linguistic studies whereas hitherto it had meant 'scientific'; entry into this cycle after 'orientation' and advice from the staff council, and a second orientation for pupils leaving the *classe de première* to enter the *classe terminale*; the gradual differentiation and therefore specialization from one of three main sections in the *classe de troisième* to one of five sections corresponding to five forms of *baccalauréat* examination. The number of hours worked in class by science pupils was slightly reduced and the timetable of the arts pupils slightly increased; their average of timetabled hours now lay between twenty-five and twenty-seven, while the technical pupils worked thirty hours. M. Fouchet did not foresee any further reduction of class time, but reiterated that the real problem was the content of the syllabus—a matter to be considered by the inspectors-general and the various education councils.

The details of this stage in the reform are of less interest than the reactions they provoked. The newspaper *Le Monde* welcomed the new equality with Latin accorded to modern languages (though it was not until after M. Fouchet's resignation in 1968 that the special place of Latin in the first cycle was abolished and a more truly common trunk of studies was planned for all sections). But various criticisms which were heard again more vociferously three years later were expressed straight away. Even *Le Figaro Littéraire*, not itself a radical journal, described the changes as a rearrangement of what already existed. 'The plan limits itself to modifying the elements of the puzzle.' The disadvantages pointed out by several commentators included too early specialization, and the fear that a choice of section made on entry into the second cycle was too likely to prove definitive. In particular, the absence of science from the curriculum of the terminal arts class was deplored. Eight points contained in a resolution passed by the Association for the Defence of Youth in School express the dissatisfaction of those chiefly concerned with curriculum rather than structures:

1. The scientific education of arts pupils was generally deficient.

2. The literary education of science pupils was diluted.

3. The creation of a new economics stream should not have been improvised.

4. The rigidity of the new system aggravated an already existing vice in school organization, viz. uncertainty in the guidance given at the end of the first cycle.

5. A barrier was being set in the way of any pupil coming from a College of General Education and hoping to enter the science stream, for he would have no second language.

6. The kind of pedagogy which had already been condemned was now being confirmed by these obligatory subjects and time-tables.

7. The periods of French in the terminal class were simply an extra burden.

8. All this damage blocked the road to effective reform.

The other main objection centred on the lack of consultation between the Minister and councils or professional bodies. This was probably a reflection of the general political style of the government which until the 1968 revolt tended to by-pass not only these bodies but the National Assembly itself. The eventual outburst of discontent and anger may have had as much to do with this exclusion from participation as with the actual decisions taken. One union of secondary school teachers placed before the Higher Council of National Education a motion deploring that the Council was expected to consider in half a day seven complicated sets of regulations, and opining that 'the brevity of time left today for the collective consideration of a set of complex and important measures is an indication of how the government views as untouchable these plans which it is only submitting to the Council in order to respect the form of the law; and the Council objects to this mock-consultation.' The organization of technical teachers objected to the idea that any authority, however exalted, could by a stroke of the pen eliminate philosophy or history from the timetable of the final technical class. The Federation of Parents asked for postponement of the reform so that the details of its application could be studied and the means found to implement it.

The teacher and the child

The struggle to establish a political relationship between the Minister and the parents is reflected in the protracted attempts to improve the pedagogical relationship between teachers and pupils. Theoretically, the method of enquiry and rediscovery, recommended by M. Brunold (Director of Secondary Education) in his circular of 6 October 1952, is increasingly adopted. The aim is

> not just to offer to pupils an account of what is known, but to show how the mind has acquired such knowledge. The procedure adopted by the mind is as important here as the goal of the study, the method as important as the results. . . . The participation of the class is then indispensable, for only the pupil who is approaching a subject that is new to him can in fact completely play the rediscovery game. Effective participation in the lesson gives the latter its true character as a set of collective investigations and enquiries, with the hesitations and errors that are inevitable and that the teacher can turn to excellent account.

Together with this approach M. Brunold recommended the 'historical method' which consists of 'presenting every situation, goal, event, problem as they presented themselves to those who first met them'. French reformers have not interpreted these recommendations to mean that pupils must be 'active' in the physical sense, or even that all teaching must be inductive from basic data and exclude deduction from principles, or that all pupils must go through in each generation the paths of discovery already trodden. Reformers want inductive as well as deductive processes, and practical attempts by pupils as well as solutions proffered by teachers. In principle, this is accepted by most teachers, but in fact difficulties arise because there is no agreed basis of psychology, no agreed concept of the curriculum in general or of the syllabus in particular, no agreed view about the use of examinations. There is too a lack of teaching material conceived for promoting active pupil participation. Most work is done from traditionally designed textbooks that cram the maximum material into the most memorable headings and sub-headings, that are dogmatic in style, raise no problems or unanswered questions, are too full and employ a complicated vocabulary.

Nor is the training of teachers yet designed to help them to resist the pressure of examinations for a school-leaving certificate or for competitive entry into the next cycle of studies. The examination is encyclopaedic in its scope, and the teacher is compelled to rapid and condensed exposition of each topic; so the pupils are cast in the role of recipients. If examinations are to be preserved, then several modifications are recommended by M. Roger Gal (1965). Candidates should only be questioned on topics that they have personally studied—not for example on the philosophy of Voltaire, or the sentiment of nature in Rousseau, or the spirit of a century. Teachers should be initiated into objective methods of assessing work done that would evoke more confidence in the pupils than does the more subjective marking of essay-type answers. They would also have to be encouraged to practice co-operation across the barriers of specialization in one's own discipline and of predetermined progress by each teacher through his own carefully timed syllabus of work. Possible modifications would be: less differentiated teaching of subjects in the elementary school, the coalescence of certain secondary school studies, for example into 'general science', and the attachment of a teacher to a class to which he or she would teach several subjects over a period of two or three years.

Here [wrote M. Gal] we touch the question of the training of teachers, which conditions everything, since teachers in general only practice with their pupils the methods to which they have themselves been used and by which they have been trained. Now the didacticism of higher education, the abuse of the delivered course of lectures, and the 'swotting' for examinations do not directly prepare them for this work. Even the training periods, for those who get them, put them into a predominantly receptive attitude and often condemn them to 'imitating' what they see being done in the classes of their teacher-counsellors. If they were to show real originality and introduce into a class a method not hitherto practiced, they would run grave risks. . . . So the absence of any physiological, psychological or sociological training leads them necessarily to emphasize the content of knowledge rather than what is happening in their pupils' minds, or what is due to the milieu in which they live, or the difficulties they meet, or the causes of failure in the individual, collectivity, family, school, character or intellect. Even the Inspectors, pressed for time, can tend to judge a teacher essentially on the qualities he shows in his exposition of facts or in the results obtained with regard to their acquisition.

The education of teachers

Not surprisingly, the reform of the teacher-training colleges has been discussed throughout the decade. As institutions for educating young primary teachers they are obsolescent. Only half the corps of primary school teachers in fact enters the profession via the *écoles normales*; the rest are taken on as unqualified assistants to a professional course in the training college, and so achieve official pensionable status. The student community of an *école normale* may thus contain adolescents recruited at the age of fifteen years to pursue their three years of study for the *baccalauréat* and their one year of professional study, and the eighteen-year-old possessors of the *baccalauréat* (mostly young women) recruited from the *lycée* for professional training, and the older experienced but unqualified candidates from the schools. It is not the homogeneous 'family' mixture of the traditional training school of pupil-teachers thriving under personal guidance and ambitious to better themselves by rising within their small township to the highest social rung accessible.

The traditional *école normale* fulfilled several social and political functions. From before the middle of the nineteenth century, when only half the population of France was French-speaking, these training schools produced the teachers who spread the French language and contributed to the unification of the country by the vigorous suppression of local dialects. In the Third Republic, the training schools staffed the expanding system of state primary schools and carried into them an anti-clerical doctrine of secularism, republicanism and radical-socialism or even socialism for which the pro-fascist Vichy Government took revenge in 1940 by closing the schools and dispersing the pupil-teachers into the *lycées*. The experience of the young teachers, competing successfully with their supposed 'betters', probably added to the ambitions of young *instituteurs* and opened a way into the primary school service via the *lycée* which is still operative.

The opening of new educational avenues means that rural young people are no longer dependent on the local all-age school for social promotion; and at the same time it means for local primary teachers the loss to secondary schools of an increasing proportion of pupils whom they might, prior to 1960, have enjoyed teaching. The primary teacher hoping to teach in a *collège d'enseignement général* might find himself less favourably considered than a young provisionally appointed student who has completed at a university that part of a degree course which entitles him to teach in a college of general education and who will in a further two years be certificated. The teacher might also be discouraged by seeing pupils whom he could have tutored carefully through a few more years of study enter the verbal abstract world of the *lycée* where family background counts so much towards academic success.

Of the hundred *écoles normales* in France, about a quarter have tried since 1963 to upgrade the professional status of the *instituteur* by offering a two-year course of post-*baccalauréat* studies. This professional cycle of studies has aroused interest as a possible prototype for future institutes in which several categories of teacher might receive specialist training—the primary school teacher, the teacher of the 'transition classes' for secondary pupils who need fostering, the teacher of the 'terminal cycle' for those who need guidance as they leave school for industry and the teacher of remedial classes for the maladjusted. The work of preparing for the *baccalauréat* would then be done either in normal *lycées* offering modern rather than classical courses, or in special pedagogical *lycées* if these were created. Such a division of the pupil-teacher's education into two cycles in two succeeding institutions is of course disputed by those who contend that the *école normale* has its own particular ethos, orientation and unity. And it is also opposed by those who uphold the goals set in the Langevin–Wallon report and look forward to the common preparation of all teachers in a university and to the degree of *licence* as the minimum qualification for them all. But some evolution or revolution in the institution will have to take place. The training schools do not supply the *Départements* with enough teachers. The schools are no longer the attractive ladder of promotion that they were in the Third Republic. All pupils will soon be following a course of secondary studies until the age of sixteen. The idea of selecting future teachers by competitive examination at the age of fifteen no longer fits with modern interpretations of 'orientation'. And since the *école normale* does not usually teach subjects outside the 'modern' course of *baccalauréat* studies, those who have taken classics or other options in that examination are not attracted to compete for entry from the *lycée*; especially, not young men. Some kind of large Departmental Institute might be a more apt institution. And in any case, some pupil-teachers are already recruited from the *lycées* after passing the *baccalauréat* examination; in the view of some directors of *écoles normales* these students are a much more lively and responsive group in the vocational classes than are the earlier entrants.

The changes would not all be gain. A vocational college satisfies some young people who want to be preparing themselves for work. A boarding college has an ethos, offers opportunity for close contact with staff and provides clubs and societies so that the personal development of young students is not totally stifled by the restricting and exhausting preparation for sitting an examination that accords more status than culture or vocational skill. But if a real sense of unity were to be preserved within these training schools, the status of the various groups of students would have to be equal. At present there prevails a hierarchy which puts primary school teachers at the bottom and then measures status by the age of the pupils to be taught, by the title of the visiting inspectorate, by the approximation of training to a post-*baccalauréat* degree, by the number of lessons to be taught each week and by the salary index of the teacher. Above the primary school pupil-teacher stand those who will leave the *école normale* equipped to teach in a college of general education, or in that general sector of a multilateral college of secondary education. One assistant-director (Delteil, 1964) of an *école normale* expressed his frustration in these terms:

> Why are we the only European country of some standing which clings to this formula of precocious recruitment and refuses to adopt another? It is humiliating to note that for twenty years our training schools have been stagnating because of resistance which may be financial, or political, or corporative.

The same commentator doubted whether the old structure is viable anyway in times when students demand both attention and freedom.

> Let us admit it. The boarding school bears the French stamp of a dual origin: the seminary and the imperial *lycée*. To give back to each institution its value or even some meaning, we should have to supply each establishment with a group of houses each supervised by a resident *professeur*. One can guess what that operation would cost financially. And one can imagine what a revolution it would be in our ways of doing things.

He went on to outline the structure of a training college for the future: recruitment from the *lycée* at the end of any second cycle of studies; vocational training for two years, plus one year of teaching practice; staff composed of specialist teachers with experience in both primary and secondary schools; a limited boarding section open only to those who needed to reside in college; co-education wherever possible; and not more than 500 students in each college.

The *Syndicat Général de l'Education Nationale*, outlining its proposals for reforms in February 1968, also argued in favour of *Instituts Universitaires de Pédagogie* which would incorporate these post-*baccalauréat* classes into a university organization responsible for the training of all teachers. Future primary school teachers would, like the others, follow a four-year course of study. This primary course would contain a large element of psychology. Teachers expecting to work in the first cycle of secondary schools, the proposed master's degree, would recognize its holder's competence in several subjects which he would teach as well as in child psychology and pedagogy. The future teachers for the upper secondary school would specialize as in the past but would also have pedagogical training. These institutes would also train future university assistant-lecturers, would find the time to do so by reducing the large number of years now spent in the preparation of doctoral theses, would give a new powerful thrust to educational psychology and would prepare future lecturers for working co-operatively as part of a departmental team in groups less dominated than at present by the immovable occupant of a professorial chair.

These are long-term goals. More immediately, the Syndicat would revive and extend the practice of organizing a two-year cycle of professional training in the *écoles normales*. This experiment started with ministerial approval but was allowed to languish. Entry to the *école normale* should be post-*baccalauréat* except for the retraining of primary school teachers who have classroom experience and who wish to specialize in work with infants, or backward pupils, or the *classes de transition* that give a general and a practical education to secondary pupils who find the normal secondary school syllabus too abstract and insufficiently orientated towards wage-earning. The post-*baccalauréat* course would form a nucleus round which the new institutes would grow and would incorporate other courses that are at present discrete: those given in *écoles normales* for future teachers in colleges of general education; those offered to students in university faculties who have declared their intention to teach and have been enrolled and sub-sidized by the university's *Institut Préparatoire à l'Enseignement du Second Degré*; and those courses followed by graduates who are studying for one year in a *Centre Pédagogique Régional* to qualify for the *Certificat d'Aptitude Pédagogique aux Enseignements du Second Degré*. Such more immediate measures could be stepping-stones towards the further goal which is the university education and peda-gogical training for all future teachers. The hope of many individuals and professional organizations working out such plans is to contri-bute to the 'inner reform' of the system by redeeming the status of the teacher, increasing the flow of recruits into the profession and supplying to the schools a corps of teachers trained for the mass education that makes more complicated demands of the profession than did the promotion of the élite.

The actual progress is of course less exciting but discernible. The number of pupil-teachers in *écoles normales* rises, and from 1968 onwards the experience of twenty-five training colleges offering a two-year professional course was accepted as valid and extended to them all. The ministerial commission on teacher-training which agreed in 1968 to this development also stipulated that the training should include preparation for the university diploma that caps the first two years of university studies. The commission declared too that the studies should be in several subjects so that each teacher would be versatile, and recommended that pedagogical training should run parallel with academic studies. The new law of November 1968 outlining the future guidelines for higher education embodied a provision for university studies to be made available to all future teachers. The eventual goal of four years of training was accepted in principle but recognized to be unattainable in the short term. For secondary school teachers the necessity of four years of study followed by one year of training was accepted too, in principle, but it was recognized that implementation would have to wait until the commission had considered the implications of this acceptance for the structure of competitive examinations at this level. *Tout se tient.*

II

A system: movement and restraint

Students' needs and others' pressures

Students are not, of course, the only pressure group: they are just among the most visible. The National Union of Primary School Teachers (*Syndicat National des Instituteurs*) has for many years pursued a policy which combined the professional advantage of its members with enlightened agitation in the forefront of the reform movement and a resentful opposition to the colleges of secondary education which might remove from primary school teachers their most attractive age-groups of pupils. Pressure for some university training can be interpreted as both properly ambitious and wisely defensive, since it would grant to non-graduate teachers the status that would secure their position as teachers in secondary schools. Meantime it is significant that in 1970 the Minister (M. Guichard) did not feel he could insist on the establishment and operation of teacher–parent councils for each primary school, although the new legislation provides for these. His restraint reflects teachers' uneasiness about their own status and practice. They are anxious not to lose the protection against local 'notables' that the system has afforded them for a century. In the past such caution was justified, for the secular representative of the State had to establish himself and defend his school from personal influence from local landowners, wealthy mayors and the *curé*. And no doubt there still exist individuals and groups who would like to exert influence upon the school. But there is also a generation of educated parents sufficiently articulate to express their children's needs and to ask for a reasonable account of the school's policy. They are likely to ask for consideration of the individual pupil, his needs and temperament, and to be dissatisfied with the pedagogy that fills the child with knowledge and demands that the child make the effort to digest and recall. So teachers are anxious, being as yet ill-prepared, and the Minister is not ready to force the issue.

Nor has rivalry between groups of teachers within the profession been absent, especially where a college of general education and a college of secondary education existed side by side in the same building, forming virtually two streams of the same school. The overall director might be a graduate *agrégé*, and the deputy-director an *instituteur* with only *baccalauréat* qualifications but with responsibilities and ambitions that set him at times above the graduate teachers. Institutional friction then heated the cold war that 'pedagogical' primary teachers and 'cultivated' graduate teachers conduct more or less continually.

One analysis (Dreyfus, 1963) of the post-war immobility in French education in fact attributed it to this inter-union squabbling, claiming that

> Parliament, under the rod of conservative *agrégés*, even when they belonged to parties of the left, opposed every reform that infringed the untouchability of the secondary school. Alongside Parliament, certain teachers' associations, in particular the *Société des Agrégés* and the *Syndicat National de l'Enseignement Secondaire* opposed all reform for the same reasons, whilst the *Syndicat National des Instituteurs* pushed for these reforms on condition that that was done for the sole benefit of its members.

As Minister of National Education in June 1967 M. Peyrefitte felt it necessary to appeal for an end to outmoded professional attitudes. 'Accept', he said to teachers, 'the inevitable renewal that you have all wished for and that you gave up hope of seeing. Overcome conservative practices: the past is dead. Stop criticizing these reforms when they are suggested to you, seeing that you called for them when you didn't have them.' For its part, the SNI passed a motion at its Congress in September 1967 condemning the government's economic, social and political policy 'inspired by power groups and employers'.

Status is relative, and the benefits of the *agrégé* are unlikely to be withdrawn or eroded. A teacher gaining this rank will retain for thirty-five or forty years his advantageous timetable, salary scale and access to a university post. To grant similar privileges to other graduates would raise the whole problem of the basis of promotion. Merit as measured by success in competitive examination has been the distinctive French principle. Any other system has always seemed to the French to open the way to favouritism or chance or to the recognition of less measurable non-academic qualities such as thrust, pedagogical skill or popularity with pupils. To abandon the scholarly standard of *agrégation* would be to question the basis of the university and one of the main instruments of republican opportunity open to all who have the talent.

Some alleviation of the examinations undergone by a candidate for this title was allowed in 1968 but in 1970 a return to normal was announced.

In the event, some of the measures introduced in 1968 to help candidates had really the opposite effect, especially in that an excessive reduction in the number of tests prevented the examiners from reaching a balanced judgment and has increased the chancy nature of the examinations.

It was also announced that, contrary to rumour, no lowering of the qualifications to candidacy would be allowed; the academic requirements and certificates or diplomas proving advanced studies beyond the level of the *licence* would be insisted upon. At the same time, having thus reaffirmed the status and quality of the *agrégés*, the Minister made a tentative move towards their professional training. 'As is known, the only training that *agrégés* received consisted of a four-weeks' course to be completed under the guidance of a *professeur* before sitting the examination. This extremely flimsy training drew criticism from all quarters; it was abolished by a decree on 2 December 1968 which envisaged in its place "pedagogical training during the first year of teaching".' The Minister then outlined his proposal for 1969–70, which was to require the heads of secondary schools to supervise newly appointed *agrégés* and ensure adequate supervision and initiation for them. Training was not required for those going to teach in universities nor for those who qualified before 1968. A more adequate form of professional training was looked forward to when the recruitment and training of secondary school teachers in general had been settled; it was still being studied.

The growing strength of pressure from teachers, parents and pupils was reflected in the proposals submitted in October 1968 to the Council of State by the Commission on School Life which the Minister had set up in July following the student riots. The commission tried to outline the conditions for 'global education' that would provide especially for 'apprenticeship in democracy', and drafted the constitution of various school committees on which various groups would be represented. *Lycées* and colleges (except colleges of general education) already had management committees, but their main function was simply to agree to the annual budget. The new administrative council for both main types of secondary school (the colleges of secondary education and general education merging in future into one multilateral secondary school, and the *lycées* confining themselves to the second cycle of studies) will be composed of school administrators, elected representatives of teachers and supervisors, as many elected representations of the school's clients (parents or older pupils) as of the teachers, the mayor, the school doctor and other co-opted citizens. Such a council might comprise up to forty-nine members, in the case of many large *lycées*, so the council will elect its own permanent executive committee to meet between the three annual sessions of the main council. A disciplinary committee is constituted by adding to the permanent executive committee the school social worker, guidance counsellor, two teachers, two representatives of the pupils, the person who raised the matter under consideration and a representative for the defence of the pupils. Former class councils now become divisional councils within the schools, and these too have representatives from the parents and the pupils.

Whether these proposals will satisfy parents and militant pupils is yet to be seen. There can be no doubt however that pressure has been violently exerted and has been responded to in such a way that a whole concept of the school as an almost closed professorial preserve has been swept away.

Pressure from the cartographers

Those who map the location of schools, determining which are to be closed and what kinds are to be built, invited themselves in 1968 to do so in accordance with certain forecasts about the school population in 1970 and certain recommendations about the nature and size of the zones from which each school will draw its intake. Each was to have its appropriate allocation of primary schools, the number of single-class schools diminishing as the school transport system grew. Each rural sector also was to have its college of general education with 400 pupils; and as the zones grew in density of population they were to be equipped with more complex secondary school systems. A 'mixed sector' with a population of up to 10,000 within a radius of ten to fifteen kilometres would have a college of secondary education receiving 600 pupils in its four sections. An 'urban sector' with a population of up to 30,000 would have a college of general education plus a college of secondary education and a first cycle of a *lycée*.

These urban sectors, grouped into 'districts' composed of ten sectors, would then be equipped with schools offering the second cycle of secondary studies. This 'district' would be large enough to supply all possible options and would then constitute an 'orientation unit'. It would offer a *lycée* with classical and modern sections; a technical *lycée* with industrial and economic sections, or an agricultural *lycée*; and a college offering two-year courses beyond the first cycle, or an agricultural college.

All this constituted, according to the Secretary-General of the Ministry, 'the applied reform'. And it must be noted that the forecasts about who was to occupy these structures were also fairly definitive. In the first cycle 55 per cent of pupils were to enter classical or modern sections of the general education course, 25 per cent were destined for transitional classes or for practical classes that would conclude their school education, 12 per cent would train for agriculture and the rest would receive special education. Thereafter 35 per cent of the age-group would follow the full three-year course and look forward to higher education, 40 per cent would follow the shorter two-year course, 8 per cent would receive special education and 17 per cent would go straight into wage-earning. The ministerial report for 1966 estimated that after deducting the small percentage for special education, about one-third of the total of each age-group was suited for practical education, the other two-thirds being considered fit for general education. Since these were the calculations according to which the school map was to be drawn, and since buildings and teachers last a long time, this kind of decision must be viewed as one of the important pressures moulding the school system.

Social, demographic and economic pressures have been referred to frequently in this study. The school explosion, that is the arrival at school of age-cohorts numbering 800,000, compelled successive Ministers to effect reforms of the school system which was designed for much smaller numbers. The pressure for democratization in the sense of admitting large numbers to truly secondary courses was a response to the injustice being done to large numbers; for while in 1956 100,000 children entered a *classe de sixième*, the same number of equally gifted children could not be received. By 1966 the number admitted to some form of secondary education (*lycée* or *CES* or *CEG*) was 530,000 (including private schools), which still represented only 60 per cent of the age-group. There was still some way to go before even the two-thirds envisaged by M. Faure could enter a secondary school (and even then the courses would vary in speed and in quality). The fear that the remaining third would founder was based on two observations. One was the nature of the teaching given in truly secondary courses. The other was the realization that for a third of the children the race is already lost by the age of eleven. The retarding influence of a road or street which cannot furnish the enrichment and stimulus enjoyed by more fortunate scholars has already had its effect: pupils and school do not match successfully.

Looking into this problem along with colleagues in the Research Department of the *Institut Pédagogique National*, M. Roger Gal (1965) recommended for these pupils less frequent changes of teacher, special remedial periods, Dienes mathematics, closer links between parents and teachers, grouping by ability in different subjects, closer observation by teachers and educational psychologists, more physical, manual and artistic activities. The Union of Secondary School Teachers (SNES), listing in 1968 the factors that would contribute to the growth of the middle school, also recognized the need for better quality in the elementary school and named that as the first of the conditions.

The importance of socio-economic factors in determining the pupil's achievement in school is fully appreciated. But the very success of the campaign for a middle school may itself weaken the primary school. The most promising student-teachers in the *écoles normales* are encouraged to go on to university, take a degree and thus move up into the secondary sector. And the most successful of the *instituteurs* are invited to a year's training course to equip them to teach in the colleges of general education that are gradually merging into colleges of secondary education. Absent teachers are replaced by less qualified substitutes. The primary sector is impoverished when it ought to be receiving fortification and renewal.

There is economic pressure too in the realm of international competition. Improvement of the primary school seems an inadequate response to the demand for increased competitiveness. The retraining of teachers and the painstaking nurture of slow learners are not matters that appeal to the politician, especially while his attention is drawn to the inadequacies of higher education. Reform in the sense of flexible syllabuses, reduced examining, sensible assessment, greater respect for applied studies and industrial efficiency was urged for example (Armand, 1967) just six months before the students' revolt,

> in the hope that in the face of new situations resulting from the Common Market and from competition on a world scale, we shall be able to draw from this intellectual élite, of which France can be proud, a higher and more differentiated output than in the preceding decades.

The new responses which students asked from their professors in 1968 and which reformers had been asking for on behalf of young pupils were certainly required for social and economic reasons; but they had to be given for pedagogical reasons, the chief of which was the respect for the learner, his needs, his anxieties and his capacity for achievement. Ministers deal more easily with buildings, examination structures, cycles and systems than with the more sensitive problems of relationships within and between institutions. It is to the interplay of these problems that we now return.

Children's needs still to be met

An inspector of primary education, M. Paul Fournier, writing in 1965 about teaching methods in the primary school, found that their chief characteristics were anxiety to produce immediate results and fear lest not enough instruction was being imparted. Pupil participation was required, but in general the teacher expounded, explained, demonstrated, manipulated, observed and summed up. This was done chiefly by words. And a large place was given to traditional pupil exercises: recitation, written homework, compositions. Hence the monotony of school life, and also the great advantage of speed in covering the ground.

The teaching method recommended by circulars issued in July and September 1963 for 'transition classes', that is to say for those pupils who had not succeeded under traditional instruction in gaining entry to the first class of secondary school, the *classe de sixième*, was to be 'active'. The children were to learn how to learn, and to proceed at their own several speeds. Since then a debate has continued over the extension or restriction of the newer methods. Why should only the slower learners have the benefit of new and stimulating methods? The answer seems to be twofold. In the first place, a group of very good pupils makes excellent progress with traditional teaching. In the second place, the new methods require teachers with enthusiasm, with a close knowledge of individual pupils and with special training in the newer techniques.

Experimental primary schools in Paris, officially designated in 1963 to co-operate with the research department of the *Institut Pédagogique National*, have tried to demonstrate the concept of the active school. This has led them to a revision of methods, to new teacher–pupil relationships, to new techniques and to a revision of the matter to be taught. The results reported in 1965 by Gloton showed the effectiveness of teamwork by the teachers, of the link between theory and practice, and of the systematic control of results. Many more pupils passed from these schools into secondary courses, where teachers commented favourably on their capacity to organize knowledge, to express themselves and to arrange their own work. Problems still to be solved included: the achievement of a balanced general education (intellectual, physical, moral and aesthetic) which would require a certain physical environment; the development of pupils beyond mere clerical skills; co-operation with parents; the balance of authority and freedom in the classroom; the firm establishment of mechanisms and knowledge by repetitive and attentive exercise.

Since the dynamic of reform does receive structural expression in such schools, why is its spread inhibited? Roger Gal, director of the research programme, named as first obstacle the encyclopaedic textbooks reflecting an overloaded syllabus. A teacher with too much to impart had to use the quickest method; and 'active' methods were thorough but initially slow. Methods which relied on learning, remembering and forgetting led, he reported (1965), to assimilation by a minority of pupils. If all were to benefit, then a distinction would have to be made between the necessary fundamentals of knowledge in any subject and other structures that would be built upon them. Official instructions, commending a syllabus and suggesting a method, have often been progressive. But the content of textbooks and the way in which teachers have felt constrained to use them in preparing pupils for examination has determined practice.

To the pressure of the syllabus was added, he found, that of examinations. The experience of the *classes nouvelles* had shown that active methods of teaching ran into greatest resistance from teachers, parents and pupils as the examination for the school-leavers' certificate approached. He proposed that pupils should only be examined on questions they had personally studied (not, for example, on the philosophy of Voltaire or on Rousseau's feeling for Nature). Teachers should be introduced to more objective forms of testing and be shown how to devise these. The syllabus should be limited, and the expectation of pupils' performance in tests should be high.

A third obstacle was the separateness of subject disciplines which prevented co-operation between teachers. Less fragmented work would have to be planned, not from the point of view of a separate subject but in relation to other subjects and also to the psychological development and interests of the pupils. This might mean the abolition in the primary school of systematic history or geography.

The education of teachers themselves was examination-bound and so didactic, said Roger Gal, that new teaching would hardly be expected from them until they had been retrained. Their emphasis was on the content of a subject, not on what is happening in their pupils' minds. The gap in their professional preparation was all the more regrettable in the case of those teachers responsible for orientation. And inspectors, pressed for time, found it easier to assess teachers for their skill in expounding knowledge or for the measured results they can show, rather than for sensitivity and understanding.

These themes were taken up again and the laments were reiterated in 1967 by Bataillon, Berge and Walter in a book conveying the findings of an organization called *Défense de la Jeunesse Scolaire*. The training of teachers, they said—recalling some of the findings of the 1966 Caen colloquium—begins when they are pupils at school; and in France that means especially the marking of individual performances whereas the colloquium was thinking more in terms of interchange—'the profession of teacher is above all relationships with others: with the pupils, with their parents, with colleagues.' It followed that the training of teachers must concern itself with the development of their personalities to a form of maturity that would conduce to classroom discussion and to an awareness of how the class as a whole is functioning as a group.

This trio of authors, trying to discuss why so much remained to be done by way of reform, found that many parents constituted a serious obstacle. Anxiety about the children's marks and place in class and prospects in examinations led parents to insist on homework even where none should officially be given and to supervise or check work already done at school under supervision in a preparation period. 'Caught in the net, they draw the mesh tighter.' Another of the strongest cords in the net was seen to be the corps of inspectors-general. They are known and recruited for brilliance of mind, and many of them have taught the post-*baccalauréat* classes preparing for entry to the *Grandes Ecoles*. Their devotion to their subject makes it difficult for them to cut the syllabus that represents so much enrichment. And their teaching experience has not led them to face the needs of average pupils in large numbers.

A contemporary perspective: students' view of the Plan

In 1968, after a period of prosperity, industrial expansion, technological development and high national prestige, a new dimension of opposition manifested itself. To students' impatience with the slow pace of reform and the halting interpretation of democratization was added their anger against the traditional constraints laid upon learners: restrictions upon their social life, passivity in reception of information, docility in accepting the purposes for which the process was designed and silence with regard to the sharing of power in the educational system and in the world. The adequacy of the national plan as an expression of national purpose was being queried, as well as its efficient implementation.

The gap between planning and control may in fact be partly due to the policies of President de Gaulle in the first decade of the Fifth Republic. The original zest of the planners was discouraged by the President's preference for more orthodox ways of building a new economy—a policy stigmatized by P. Mendès-France (1968) as 'deplanification or the abdication of the State to the advantage of the market'. This view coincides with that of F. C. Gruson who argued before the unrest of May–June 1968 that nobody had really taken seriously the need for adequate planning techniques and for adequate organization of collective deliberation and of powers. The last complaint points again to the breakdown of consultation, transmission, debate and representatives' power in the National Assembly, that many commentators have referred to in their studies of the Fifth Republic. 'Failure', he wrote with considerable pre-science,

> will become progressively manifest when—as economic
> development emerges from the developmental perspectives that
> had formerly been foreseen for it—the structures resulting from
> long-term decisions taken in the past will be ill-adapted to the
> existing situation and will lead either to grave political disorders
> or to waste, a halt to growth, and retreat from the solution of
> great political problems.

Reviewing in November 1968 his policy, when presenting his proposed education budget for 1969, M. Faure told the National Assembly that 'the Plan itself has been seriously outstripped by the evolution of and the consequences of measures taken in other fields.' In fact, the whole structure designed to prolong schooling to the age of sixteen years had broken down. In theory pupils should have gone on to technical schools or continued in a *lycée*; but in fact many simply had to stay on in technical classes that were not even 'secondary' in type. Nor had the experiment of part-time industrial training in firms' apprenticeship schemes proved satisfactory. The Plan had been invalidated, he claimed, not because it was badly conceived but because reality did not run always in the prepared channels. Reality presented, in this case, some particularly obstinate aspects. Technical education—despite the abolition of a special Branch in the Ministry—remained too separate from general education, was presented as an unfamiliar option and was viewed still as a second-class course. A second obstacle was the number of pupils still apparently unready for secondary education and in need of remedial courses to help them catch up. And M. Faure also felt the need to defend as valid and truly cultural a form of education that did not contain Latin. To view it as inferior was, he said, a serious error whose repercussions were felt at university level in the shortage of students in scientific and technical establishments. He proposed certain structural changes—the rapid merging of colleges of general education with colleges of secondary education, a year of remedial studies for some adolescents, the introduction of various arts and crafts into the general curriculum and lots of gangways in the upper school to enable pupils to pass from general to technical courses—but the details are probably less significant than the fact that the moulds had been admitted to be inadequate and that any future plans would have to take into account some intractable pedagogical facts.

In this way the changes which we mentioned at the beginning of this study were effected. They were changes within the limits set by the administrative structure, by the primacy of the traditional culture and by the association with these factors of certain groups in social and political life. Some adjustment of examination subjects, of selection procedures, of syllabuses and methods and of qualifications for entry into higher courses of study; some further upgrading of technical studies and of technical schools, which are not so clearly a denominational sphere of influence as the private *lycées* and colleges, and which must be encouraged if France is to keep power and the sort of prestige it brings: these sorts of reform were proposed in 1955, discarded as inadequate by M. Billères in 1956 and 1957 and enacted by decree in January 1959.

Since then the administrative structure has been adapted several times, but complaint has continued about under-administration. The necessity of unified central control based in Paris is questioned; autonomy and regionalization are terms that have acquired new power. The lack of professional administrators in the Ministry of National Education is repeatedly mentioned. Critics would like to see more interpretation of policy to the public and consultation with the public; and these may only have come about recently as a result of the catastrophic upheavals that Langevin hoped to avoid. For there has been confusion in reform. One step has not always been followed by the next. Changes in examination structures have been made and retracted, or have been made so suddenly and with such inadequate preparation, as in 1967, that students felt insecure and aggrieved. Some reforms, stretching over a long period of trial or of building, such as the new relationships between Church and State, or the development programme for colleges of secondary education, have not caused disruption and may, given time and a favourable political climate, establish themselves.

The first significant pruning of a syllabus was achieved in 1967 when the mathematics programme for two final classes in secondary schools was lightened by the removal of over a quarter of the material. These topics were deemed by the (initially unofficial) Lichnerowicz commission to be superfluous, and the retraining of teachers in the new mathematics was begun. One consequence of vigorous innovation is illustrated by this quotation from the Ministry's report for 1967.

> The arrangement and renovation of textbooks undertaken after the 1966 changes in structures and curricula have continued, especially in the field of mathematics, for the second, first and terminal classes. Textbooks have also been prepared for those classes in the first cycle in which experiments are being made in the teaching of modern mathematics. (*Le Mouvement éducatif en France*, 1967.)

The movement for reform continues, but an uneasy relationship exists between the experimenters and the administration which should generalize their results. In 1964, for example, the *Défense de la Jeunesse Scolaire* investigated the teaching of French grammar; an official Circular took note of the recommendations and promised further action; a committee prepared new Instructions for teachers; but these were then remitted to a wider commission dealing with the reform of primary education as a whole (Bataillon, Berge and Walter, 1967). According to the official report for 1967, 'experiments are now being made with a primary education taken out of its isolation (*cycle élémentaire désenclavé*); the pedagogic unit is no longer the class but the whole elementary cycle during which pupils learn fundamental mechanisms which will permit them to speak, to write, and to discover certain mathematical concepts.' This may be an attempt by the Ministry to introduce new teaching into new structures. The movement for the Defence of Youth in School expressed itself less hopefully on general tactics. 'Everything happens as if our choice were only between immobility and ill-considered action. Up till now, it has almost always been one or the other.'

Seen in this light the revolutionary activity of some students in 1968 can be understood as an attempt to break the mould in the hope that whatever forces were then released would be healthy and growing. The political interpretation of reform—changes not too surely introduced (and not too clearly related to any coherent time-table or plan) as pressures become irresistible at successive levels—had in their view proved inadequate and irrelevant. It had not yet translated 'democratization' (the politicians' own aim) into insti-tutional terms. It had not dynamically swept away obstacles. It had not provided new channels for new forces that were bursting with grievance and idealism while politicians were trying to cope with problems set by a previous decade or century. Various Ministers were aware of the need both to plan a coherent general reform, since each adjustment affected adjacent parts of the system, and to move step by step; but they had supposed that this was the chief tension to be resolved—the tension between the ideological reformer and the pragmatic politician with limited resources. The danger was then interpreted to be the bursting of structures subjected to demo-graphic or social pressures. Until 1968 this was a problem for the politician, not a threat to the government. The appropriate response was deemed to be an alteration of such structures as the arrange-ments for entry into secondary schools, the succession of cycles, the optional subjects in examinations, the hierarchy of certificates, dip-lomas and degrees. When the Minister declared 'all our structures have burst' he was thinking in terms of building provision, staff recruitment, study programmes, *baccalauréat* degrees and arrange-ments of that kind. Successive governments took a series of actions some of which derived from the Decree of January 1959 and some from the movement of the wave of pupils through the various levels of school. Some general intent—an approximation to a middle school characterized by a common general education and progressive orien-tation—was discernible.

But the reforms within the secondary schools were not sufficient. Increasingly, research showed that advantage and disadvantage stemmed from the poverty or richness of a child's family background, and that reform must compensate early in school life for any social handicap. And at the upper end of the educational process, it became apparent that a diversity of outlets must be provided if student 'failures' were not to be inhumanly discarded. Such provision must include new colleges or institutes, and new links with industry, and must be offered as counsel or guidance or orientation; but it must not be so compelling as to limit a student's sense that to some important extent his vocation was his own choice.

A new dimension: students' reaction to the mould

In another sense too the reforms achieved before 1968 were inadequate. They had been 'structural'. But the model of society as a structure or a series of structures is an analogy and it breaks down in some situations. Society can also be seen as a complex of relationships and power differentials in a perpetual state of flux, and it may only bear a resemblance to a structure in so far as at any given time there is a number of expectations which is widely held and a corresponding number of obligations recognized (Swaisland, 1969).

What students and *lycéens* and some teachers and parents and groups dedicated to reform have tried to change is the relationship between teachers and taught, and the power differential between the governors and the governed. The calm of the university has been disturbed and will not easily be restored, for teachers (including those who have striven for reform) find their authority disturbingly questioned. Their personal adequacy is under examination by their students and by themselves. And those who govern (and who have always claimed to be promoting reform) have to reconcile the requirements of public order with the need to appear to accept the dynamic of reform.

Meantime new relationships have been encouraged by the constitution of work parties and of administrative councils on which students and pupils and parents and teachers are represented. The hope of the government is that these new arrangements will come to be new 'structures', that the students will play the game, accepting the rules of committee discussion and the implied expectations and obligations. If they do not, then the new structures too can be said to break down, or be inadequate or be violently demolished—according to one's point of view—and new relationships for discussion and the exercise of power will emerge from the conflict.

In a period of rapid expansion, when students (or pupils) and staff are entering institutions whose traditional expectations they only partly share, disruption has occurred. Some institutions have been too rigid, some too slowly flexible and some new ones have inherited characteristicst hat are difficult to modify. In France the policy of the much more open secondary school and the very open university eliminates the possibility of control by selective recruitment. Young people have entered secondary courses who needed teaching, guidance and studies not traditionally offered. And students, entering university in greater numbers, are no longer content just to have 'had their chance' in the first years and to drop quietly out if they fail to pass through the internal sifting system. They have demanded both respectful treatment as adults, who are aware of their worth, and remunerative outlets commensurate with their graduate status even if society in general does not yet want to employ large numbers of sociologists and psychologists.

An important element in this disturbance of set patterns has been the 'infection' of the *lycéens* by the students. Of course it must be remembered that some *lycées* retain the best candidates for the *Grandes Ecoles* and prepare them after the *baccalauréat* examination during the following two years. So the age ranges of *lycéens* and students overlap. But the younger group too were active in demonstrations against war in Vietnam and then against police intervention in what were regarded as student affairs. So the training of these future students has been for political participation, demonstration, strikes, sit-ins, working parties and boycotts as well as for serious academic study. And in much of this they were supported in the summer of 1968 by the strike action of their teachers. The new student will not just study; he will also have political opinions on national and university government. And he may query the traditional neutrality of investigation, research and teaching—preferring some form of commitment and involvement as stimuli to his thought. Neutrality in France was a safeguard against open recurrence of the State–Church dispute or of the Monarchist–Revolutionary dispute, both of which are of little interest to the rising generation though they still dominate the thought of those in control. For the new students, criticism of society is a right, even if the students are among the many who want chiefly to work for examinations and a qualification and a profession. In this respect the French students were probably following fairly consistently the example of their teachers who analyse and criticize society academically; and the students applied similar criteria to the institutions they know most closely.

The teachers themselves were split, and this did not make for easy acceptance of traditional university values by the students. Teachers defended simultaneously their own privileged status as *agrégés* and the concept of '*culture générale*'. They too had been known to strike in defence of their powers. And the most highly qualified of them academically were those who had least preparation for communicating with students or pupils. As examples to the young, many were noticeably absent, leaving the school or amphitheatre after the class or lesson and giving little time to extracurricular contact. Their defence was of course the time needed for preparation, research, further qualification or promotion and the control of examinations. But examinations were queried by some students as an unwelcome form of social control, and in boycotting them even temporarily students were refusing the *rites de passage* into a society that looked unattractive.

The disturbances that started in 1968 have been referred to as pseudo-revolution and psycho-drama. This latter term at least needs to be taken seriously. Students were obviously under strain, and some release was sought. The patterns were to hand in revolts that had taken place elsewhere and had shown how to demonstrate and how to make numbers tell. The Paris version of student reaction to strain included barricades. The provincial uprisings demonstrated very significantly the operation of an autonomous university in Strasbourg and of temporary regional control by a coalition of students and strikers in Nantes. Politically these operations did not last. But if they correspond to some psychological need of young people to take control, to talk, to work out constitutions and to assert themselves in ways more adult and politically dangerous than students' 'rags', then the psycho-drama must be taken seriously too.

Their grievances show how tightly one aspect of the system is linked to another so that a reformer must end by attacking the system. A teaching method which appeals only to a minority acts as a restraint on the achievement of a social aim by frustrating further progress towards democratization. So does an examination system which retards a large percentage of pupils and lets only a restricted percentage through to higher education. But if more get through as the restrictions are relaxed in schools, should selection then be operated by universities? Student organizations oppose it and politicians avoid the word 'selection', but the new University Law made provision for 'orientation courses' to be followed by those students whose qualifications are doubtful. At the conclusion of his course the student will be 'guided' as to his next step. If he declines to follow discouraging advice and then fails his examination at the end of the year then he must either withdraw or undergo another orientation course. So the enormous flow of students into universities—twice as many as in the more selective British universities—continues and so does the process of distribution from the flow, so that France and Britain produce in the end comparable numbers of graduates. France has opted to solve the problems set by orientation rather than those set by selection. The choice is not the one that all academics would have made, but it is politically viable. It is also acceptable to the school system, because the whole apparatus of teaching for the *baccalauréat* need not be dismantled. Students and teachers concur, so far, in the operation of a system which is traditional, egalitarian, fairly predictable in its results from year to year, and reflects the nationally accepted practice of promotion by examination from one category or class to the next. To upset the system would be to question a basic tenet of French public administration. Yet the function of a normal examination in school and university, as opposed to the competitive examination for a restricted admission or qualification or promotion, is being questioned. It is now suggested that guidance should be so well done that 80 per cent of students entering upon a cycle of studies should complete it successfully. Without the degree of hope and confidence the examination falls as a shadow between teacher and taught.

This is the shadow of non-participation, the darker side of a carefully organized system of examinations and certificates. In schools it manifests itself as non-co-operation, as a sort of sullen resentment and occasionally as an outburst of noisy indiscipline. The teacher who has been working to fill his passive pupils with information, who expects both submission and their eager response when invited to emulate each other, who must too often classify his pupils by allocating a mark and communicate with them chiefly when hearing their recitation of a learned lesson, is protected from the strains of inter-personal contact; but is open to the charge of avoiding it, of being unwilling to meet and converse with pupils.

These were the charges so often heard in *lycées* and universities in May 1968. They are associated with a system that depends upon impersonal assessment of achievement, that has only recently introduced more personal and continuous evaluation, that needs to 'mark' precisely and that must therefore set a syllabus and questions that can be reduced to measurable data. The curriculum is taught abstractly, verbally, precisely. The machinery of examination needs constant maintenance and minor adjustment but seems not to be able to cope with the pressures of large numbers of aspiring articulate students conscious of their power. When the students reject the social position for which this education had prepared them, then the whole system is questioned, pupils riot and threaten not to sit their examinations, a crisis is recognized; and the necessary adjustments are made to enable the system to start functioning again.

The students' hostility towards 'the system' and the bureaucracy indicates how the educational institutions are seen as characteristic of general State structures. The chain of association is described by Crozier (1964, p. 243).

> The French bureaucratic model requires high educational standards because it must meet somewhat contradictory aims. It must train young people for the different and difficult roles of a complex industrial society, select them for entering the higher strata by completely impersonal methods, and yet prevent the social status quo from being upset by an overly rapid social mobility.

So the competition involved in such selection and the consequently heavy burden of learning designed to elicit the élite were diagnosed by hostile students and are still interpreted by reformers as elements in a system that is both educational and political. To attack the State through the University is not so irrational. Nor is it surprising that Ministers, since 1968, have been building defences for the State by introducing reforms into the educational system. Teachers are urged to base their teaching on the life experience of their pupils rather than upon written accounts. The pupil and his needs and his growth are central to the process, rather than the subject and its academic structure. Teachers and pupils are to engage in face-to-face relationships. Admission to a cycle of studies implies a strong presumption that successful completion will be achieved. Irreversible selection is delayed. Syllabuses are lightened and more time is allowed for mastery of their content.

It is just possible that in the processes of planning too, some significant movement is visible that cannot be reversed. Planning no longer takes into account only quantities, fair shares, recruitment of resources and manpower needs but also the qualities of operations. New planning groups within the Ministry, new professional categories such as educational counsellors, new grades of teachers whose status cannot easily be determined in traditional terms, new consultation councils in which parents and students are vocal— all these tend to break up old groupings and to have a renovating effect. Students' and citizens' groups organized for reform have demonstrated significant patterns of co-operative action and have made demands upon the State that the old machinery cannot meet. The educational system was already under-administered, and is now so over-extended that it cannot respond to the demands for local school transport, local relationship between schools and job opportunities, local links between the school curriculum and the environment, local initiative in arranging societies, excursions and so on. It has had to declare a policy of decentralization. This is a very important reversal of the administrative policy that has prevailed in France since the seventeenth century, and it is not likely to be implemented as easily as the word is uttered by Ministers.

The system is under pressure but the politicians cannot start from zero. It is the present system that they have to alter. It cannot just be swept away and replaced by an ideal blueprint, yet the new vision must be preserved and fostered. So the Minister has to make reforms piecemeal while calling for a new mentality that will keep the reform movement in motion without upsetting structures. The experience of a decade indicates that while the system is not immobile, the rate of adaptation to new pressures and new demands is so unsatisfactory that periodical recourse must be had to measures which are outside the administrative and the normal parliamentary procedure. Crisis occurs and during the upheaval some groups win what advantage they can by way of monetary reward or institutional recognition. Power is redistributed and the machinery is restarted. Conservative forces reassert themselves, professional groups assert their rights and defend themselves against new pressures. But the machinery needs overhaul and modernization at so many points that partial breakdown must recur frequently until the system acquires a new flexibility. So while the Minister has declared a dual policy—progressive reform by law and administration, concurrently with the proclamation of new principles—his introduction of parents into decision-making councils and his introduction of 'renewal' into the pedagogy of institutions have both met with the resistance of inertia in those for whom change means loss of power and diminished authority.

Nor is the new ideology bound to succeed. Decentralization removes the locus of some decision-making, but while the departmental Prefects are closer than Parisian officials to the feelings of local citizens, they are not initiators of policy. They supply the data according to which the school map is drawn, but they are not long-term planners. Their consultative committees offer a good forum for confrontation, but it is not at the level of the *département* that major grievances are removed. While most power remains at the centre, that is where revolt will be directed.

The principles emunciated by M. Guichard before the Senate in the autumn of 1969 were participation, autonomy and the mixture of academic disciplines. Speaking of the first, he looked forward to the new stability that might develop as new committee members became responsible.

If to begin with the co-opted personalities have to be technical experts rather than co-partners, yet their collaboration will open perspectives, suggest forms of support, stimulate financial contributions which gradually will provide a substantial basis for co-operation and will transform it into co-responsibility. Likewise, the entrance of students into councils will lead them to take account of pedagogical necessity and to replace the subordination of education to academic subjects by the subordination of subjects to education: it will become possible to find one's way among forms of schooling that have thus acquired a purpose and the notion of a study contract may emerge. . . . On the other hand, it is not undermining the confidence necessary for smoothly functioning participation if I clearly mark out certain limits. Let it be clearly understood that four areas remain the preserve of teachers alone: the choice

of their peers, the judgment of their peers, the choice of
direction for their research, and examinations.

On the subject of financial autonomy granted to the new universities,
M. Guichard had this to say,

> The role of the university council will be to share out among
> the teaching and research units . . . the global allocations set by
> the Ministry after consultation with the National Council for
> Higher Education and Research. So the Council will be
> responsible for a real educational policy. No doubt the allocation
> of the total grant will be encompassed by recommendations,
> but the freedom of action enjoyed by the university will be
> beyond all comparison with that of the former Faculties,
> tied as they were by a budget drawn up in Paris item by item
> and by strict *a priori* control. This freedom even seems
> dangerous to some who fear local empires and who prefer the
> uncertain guardianship of a distant and overworked Ministry;
> and these fears explain the opposition met by certain marriages
> which are however necessary for the constitution of the new
> universities.

On the subject of pedagogical autonomy, the Minister defended
freedom to teach in one's own way and reaffirmed national control
over the content of professional and competitive national examinations. The unwilling marriages mentioned by the Minister refer to
the reluctant fusion of dissimilar Faculties into multi-disciplinary
'teaching and research units'. A change of outlook is necessary if
these are to be reconstituted and then to be viable so that a student
may follow a course of studies in the first cycle and then choose a
more specialized course from several that are made available without
jettisoning a large part of the knowledge he has already acquired.
The Minister was only too well aware of the restraints that had
operated as the universities reconstituted themselves in accordance
with the new law.

> In the past year, as you know, 630 teaching and research units
> have been constituted out of existing Faculties and provisional
> administrative councils have replaced the traditional committees.
> It must be said that this method has not facilitated the
> establishment of really new universities: very often, the old

Faculties have divided themselves artificially into teaching and research units and reconstituted themselves at the level of the administrative councils.

But he did not propose to go back and start again.

So in the interplay of power exercised by government and institutions and citizens sometimes one is dominant and sometimes another. A whole system was set up to protect the citizen against local powers and to offer him access to the ladder of promotion. For some it worked. For many the system became in turn an obstacle rather than a staircase because the university became rigidly devoted to abstract deductive thought purveyed in academic disciplines in classrooms where personal encounter between student and teacher was largely confined to the intellectual transmission of information. To break the system a President and Minister with full powers of government were necessary, but even they were restrained in their action and a more violent outburst from the third of the parties concerned was required before the urgency of reform was widely recognized. The new university law came again from the top and ran into the resistance of established forms. The momentum of reform diminished, although the purposes were avowedly democratic, so that the system could maintain some stability. And the discontent has continued to rumble and to threaten with the new power, articulateness and rights to participation that had been acquired. So long as power and participation and initiation pass uneasily from partner to partner the machinery will operate jerkily. The new 'contract' between them is still in the drafting stage and the process is not purely verbal. Reaction is more immediate and less easily overlooked than in the decade of the sixties. Whether the adjustment to feed-back will be sensitive and speedy will determine in large measure the size and frequency of crises in the seventies.

Suggestions for further reading

ARDAGH, J. 1968. *The New French Revolution*, Secker & Warburg. A social and economic survey of France, 1945–67

CHARLTON, D. G. 1963. *Secular Religions in France 1815–70*, OUP. A study of the nineteenth-century sources of modern French secular thought

CROS, L. 1962. *L'explosion scolaire*, Sevpen. An examination of demographic and social trends affecting French education

DUVEAU, G. 1957. *Les Instituteurs, Editions du Seuil.* A study of the French primary school teacher, his history and his concept of a mission

GREEN, F. C. 1965. *French and British Civilization 1850–1870*, Dent. A comparative study of the ideas and tastes that characterize two civilizations

HOFFMAN, S., *et al.* 1963. *France: Change and Tradition*, Gollancz. Six writers examine and illustrate various aspects of modern France

RIDLEY, F., and BLONDEL, J. 1964. *Public Administration in France*, Routledge & Kegan Paul. A study of government administration and of the organization of various departments including the Ministry of National Education

WILLIAMS, P. M. 1968. *The French Parliament (1958–1967)*, George Allen & Unwin. An account of constitutional and political conditions in the Fifth Republic

Bibliography

ALAIN, 1938 *Propos sur l'éducation*, Paris: Rieder
ARMAND, L. 1967 in *Education Nationale*, 14 December 1967
ARON, R. 1968 *La Révolution Introuvable*, Paris: Fayard
ARRA, M. 1957 in *Education Nationale*, 14 November 1957
Avenirs, May–June 1959, Paris: Bureau Universitaire de Statistique et de Documentation Scolaires et Professionnelles.
BARON, R. 1968 in *Education Nationale*, 24 October 1968
BATAILLON, M., BERGE, A., and WALTER, F. 1967 *Rebâtir l'Ecole*, Paris: Payot
BAZIN, R. 1963 in *Education Nationale*, 7 November 1963
BERTHOIN, J. 1959 in *Education Nationale*, 8 January 1959
BOUTET DE MONVEL, A. 1961 in *Education Nationale*, 21 September 1961
BOYANCE, R. 1957 in *Le Figaro Littéraire*, 15 June 1957
BRUNOLD, C. 1960 in *Education Nationale*, 23 June 1960
—— 1952 *Mémoires et Documents Scolaires*, Paris: Ministère de l'Education Nationale
BUISSON, F. 1911 *Nouveau dictionnaire de pédagogie et d'instruction primaire*, Paris: Hachette; quoted by Palméro, J. (1955), *Histoire des Institutions et Doctrines Pédagogiques*, Paris: SUDEL
CAPELLE, J. 1966 *L'Ecole de demain reste à faire*, Paris: Presses Universitaires de France
—— 1967 *Tomorrow's Education: the French experience*, Oxford: Pergamon Press, tr. W. D. Halls
CAPLAT, G. 1960 *L'administration de l'éducation nationale et la réforme administrative*, Paris: Berger Levrault
CHATEAU, J. 1957 i in *Education Nationale*, 9 May 1957
—— ii *Ecole et Education*, Paris: J. Vrin
CHATREIX, H. 1946 *Au-delà du laïcisme—ou la paix scolaire*, Paris: Editions du Seuil
CHRISTOPHER, J. B. 1951 'Desiccation of the bourgeois spirit' in *Modern France* (ed. E. Earle), Princeton University Press
CLARKE, F. 1933 in *Year Book of Education*, Evans Brothers
Communist Party of France 1967 *L'Ecole et la Nation*, no. 156, February 1967
COURNIL, P. 1959 in *Cahier Reconstruction*, September 1959
—— i quoting official *Informations Statistiques* for March 1958
—— ii quoting *Document 189*, June 1959, from the Ministry of National Education

174

CRÉMIEUX-BRILHAC, J-L. (ed.) 1965 *L'Education Nationale*, Paris: Presses Universitaires de France

CROS, L. 1960 i Introduction to the *Encyclopédie pratique de l'éducation en France*, Paris: Institut Pédagogique National

—— ii in *Education Nationale*, 2 June 1960

—— 1956 in *Education Nationale*, 8 November 1956

—— 1959 in *Education Nationale*, 29 May 1959

CROZIER, M. 1964 *The Bureaucratic Phenomenon*, Tavistock Publications

DELTEIL, E. 1964 in *Education Nationale*, 28 May 1964 and 11 June 1964

DREYFUS, G. 1967 *Rapport aux Assises Générales de l'U.N.R.-U.D.T.*

—— 1963 *Rapport aux Assises Générales de l'U.N.R.-U.D.T.*

ELLUL, J. 1957 in *Réforme*, 3 August 1957

Esprit June 1954 Paris

—— May–June 1964 Paris

FAUVET, J. 1957 *La France Déchirée*, Paris: Arthème Fayard

FÈBVRE, L. 1950 Preface to Friedmann G., *Humanisme du Travail et Humanités*, Paris: Armand Colin

Fédération Protestante de l'Enseignement 1957 *Laicité et Paix Scolaire*, Paris: Berger-Levrault

FERRY, G. 1954 in *Esprit*, June 1954, p. 943

—— 1968 in *Education Nationale*, 19 April 1968

FOURASTIÉ, J. 1962 in *Education Nationale*, 1 February 1962

FOURNIER, P. 1965 in *Education Nationale*, 14 January 1965

FRAISSE, P. 1954 in *Esprit*, June 1954

—— 1959 in *Esprit*, October 1959

GAL, R. 1965 *Courrier de la Recherche Pédagogique*, no. 26, pp. 2–29

—— 1957 in *Year Book of Education*, Evans, pp. 235–6

—— 1959 in *Education Nationale*, 9 April 1959

GAUSSEN, F. 1968 in *Le Monde*, 27 March

GLOTON, R. 1965 *Courrier de la Recherche Pédagogique*, September 1965

GROSSER, A. 1968 article in *Le Monde*

GRUSON, F. C. 1968 *Origine et espoirs de la planification française*, Paris: Dunod

HÉBERT, J. P. 1954 in *Esprit*, June 1954

HIGNETTE, M. 1956 'The Primacy of the Rational in French Education', *Year Book of Education 1956*, Evans

HUBERT, R. 1949 *Histoire de la Pédagogie*, Paris: Presses Universitaires de France, pp. 53–4

Institut Pédagogique National 1970 i *L'organisation de l'Enseignement en France*

—— ii *L'Enseignement Supérieur*

International Yearbook of Education, annually Geneva: International Bureau of Education, and Paris: Unesco

KANDEL, I. L. 1959 *The New Era in Education*, Harrap

KERLEVEO, J. 1956 *L'Enseignement libre, service privé d'intérêt général en droit public français*, Paris: Secrétariat Général de l'enseignement libre

LEGRAND, L. 1963 in *Education Nationale*, 13 October 1963

LENOIR, T. 1959 in *L'Express*, 1 January 1959

LIZOP, E. 1957 in *Revue des Deux Mondes*, 15 September 1957

MADELIN, L. *La Nation sous l'Empereur*, Paris: Hachette, quoted 1955 by Palméro J., *Histoire des Institutions et Doctrines Pedagogiques*, Paris, SUDEL

MAJAULT, R. 1967 *La Révolution de l'Enseignement*, Paris: R. Laffont

MALRIEU, R. 1965 in *Education Nationale*, 18 February 1965

MARCHAIS, J. 1956 in *Education Nationale*, 8 November 1956

MASSÉ, P. 1961 quoted in *Economic Planning in France*, PEP, vol. xxvii, no. 454

MAUROIS, A. 1955 *Portrait de la France et des Français*, Germany: Langewiesche-Brandt

MENDÈS-FRANCE, P. 1968 in *Le Monde Hebdomadaire*, 7–13 November 1968

MERLE, M. 1964 in *Esprit*, May–June 1964, p. 935

MONOD, G. 1954 in *Esprit*, June 1954

MORAZÉ, C. 1957 quoted by Fauvet J., in *La France Déchirée*, Paris: Fayard, p. 35

PERRET, J. 1968 *Inquiète Sorbonne*, Paris: Hachette

POIGNANT, R. 1962 in *Education Nationale*, 15 February 1962

Political and Economic Planning, *Economic Planning in France*, vol. xxvii, no. 454, p. 227

REUCHLIN, M. 1966 in *Education Nationale*, 3 February 1966

ROBERT, F. n.d. *L'humanisme : essai de définition*, Paris: BUDET

SIEGFRIED, A. 1951 'Approaches to an Understanding of Modern France', in *Modern France* (ed. E. Earle), Princeton University Press

SWAISLAND, C. 1969 quoted from a lecture delivered at Woodbrooke College, Birmingham

THABAULT, R. 1957 in *Year Book of Education*, 1957, Evans, p. 554

THIBAUDET, A. 1932 *Les Idées Politiques de la France*, Paris: Librairie Stock

VIAL, F. 1936 *Trois Siècles d'Histoire de l'Enseignement Secondaire*, Paris: Delagrave

WILLIAMS, P. 1954 *Politics in Post-War France*, Longmans

WITTENBERG, A. 1961 in *Education Nationale*, February–March 1961 and May 1961

Index